THE RESURRECTOR

THE
RESURRECTOR

MOSHE MIKANOVSKY

NEW DEGREE PRESS

THE RESURRECTOR

ISBN

978-1-63730-810-3   *Paperback*

978-1-63730-872-1   *Kindle Ebook*

978-1-63730-978-0   *Digital Ebook*

To Hagit, Daniella, Avigail, and Talia.

You are the reason I can do this every day.

My love. Always and forever.

And You are trustworthy to resurrect the dead.

—GEVUROT, DAILY *AMIDA*, THE JEWISH PRAYER BOOK

A thin strand of saliva falls from his mouth to the ocean, and all the continents on either side await only him. Such is my son: anything less than a whole world, he will not dream of.

—*THE CONSTANT MOURNER*, HANOCH LEVIN
TRANSLATED BY JESSICA COHEN
AND EVAN FALLENBERG

AUTHOR'S NOTE

———

The story of *The Resurrector* is fictional, unless you believe that someone can come back to life. All characters and their stories are a complete work of fiction and came from my imagination. If they remind you of someone you know, it is merely a coincidence.

But *do* you believe in some type of resurrection? Part of the book is just that —"What if?" When I read works of fiction, I always try to find the nugget in the core of it all, the question that the author explored when writing the story. These can be extreme life situations or magical ones. And this was my "what if": What if someone can bring back someone from the dead? Would it change anything for their loved ones? The obvious answer is, of course, it would. Near death experiences change people's perspective on life, making them appreciative of the important things they have and focus on them.

But let's think about it a bit deeper... Would it? If they had their issues before, would they be able to overcome them just like that? Egos, belief systems, social pressures—these all can be stronger than, well, death.

So, I started exploring. I placed it in the environment I know, my homeland Israel and home-city, the religion I was born into and grew up in, and my childhood and adulthood, and the characters started forming themselves. They started interacting with each other and with their environment. Words came into their mouths and thoughts in their heads. It was important for me to keep them authentic. While I have lived for the past twenty-five years in North America, I wanted to ensure the characters and their story do not lie. They had to be true to the place and people I love. My hope is that I showed them justice. It's hard to do in stories. They are limited to their themes, and the story has to move forward.

But in too many Israeli stories, both in books and movies, the focus is mostly on the extreme. The Israeli-Palestinian conflict. The ultra-ultra-orthodox person who leaves the religion. The Holocaust survivors and the generational gaps with their descendants. Some do appear in *The Resurrector* as well, but they are not the main focus, and I hope they do not overshadow the main theme—that family relationships and love are for here and now, for the living. Let's not wait until it is too late. And this theme, my friend, is eternal. It has no culture or religion. It is here for you and everyone on earth, no matter our background, the deity we believe in, what we look like within and without. This is what makes us human.

So here I bring to you *The Resurrector*, a story that is rooted in time and place but unrooted in thought and feelings. It has some mystery. It has some magic. But most of all, it is a work of love.

I hope you enjoy it.

Toronto Ontario, 2013-2021

Forewarning: This story includes some adult content and themes.

For dictionary of Hebrew and Jewish terms mentioned in the book, please visit author.mikanovsky.com/the-resurrector-dictionary or scan the following QR code.

PROLOGUE

Friday

"Abba, *shalom*." Ram took a deep breath, the phone handset pushing hard into the palm of his hand.

"Ram? Hi, how are you? What a pleasant surprise! I was just thinking about you." That was his father's usual greeting. It had been a week since they last spoke, and his father sounded the same as always.

"I'm okay. But I don't know what is going on with Nir. He—"

Before he had a chance to continue, Chaim erupted on the other end of the line. "You know I don't want to hear his name or discuss him! Why do I even have to remind you? Just don't mention him to me." His words were clipped and abrupt.

Ram imagined his father standing in his kitchen by the counter, a coffee mug in one hand, the daily paper spread out in front of him, forgotten, the cordless phone in his other hand, a thick vein bulging at his temple.

"You have to hear me this time!" Ram shouted into the phone, angry with his father for never listening. "He is missing!" It was not how he planned to say it.

The line went quiet. His father didn't hang up, but he didn't say anything either. Ram's pulse was beating hard like a drum in his ears. His hand sweaty, he switched the phone to his other hand, wiping the sweat off on his army uniform pants. Ram told Chaim everything that happened since his sister, Millie, called hysterical from her *ulpena* high school after waiting for hours for their brother Nir to show up. He spoke quickly, afraid his father would stop him mid-sentence. When he finished, Ram paused to breathe and to collect his thoughts.

A long silence on the line. What more could he say?

"Are you still there, Abba?" Ram checked the phone, but this was an old-fashioned rotary unit at his army base, with no way to know if the line was still connected.

"What is the policeman's name?"

Ram gave the information to his father, who took it silently and promised to call Officer Sela.

"Thank you, Abba. I am coming to Tel Aviv tonight. I got a pass from my commander for a few days so I can search for Nir. I will sleep in the house if that's okay."

"Tonight? Do you know what day it is?" Chaim asked.

At first, Ram did not register the meaning of the question. Then, he remembered: it was Friday. He glanced at his watch and made a quick calculation in his head. If he had a car he could make it before sundown with some time to spare. But he did not own a car, and it would probably take him much longer to arrive in Tel Aviv. He made up his mind.

"I can borrow a car from the base. Don't worry," he said. He could live with the lie, especially given that Nir's whereabouts were at stake.

"You won't make it."

"I will," Ram insisted.

"What good would it do? You will get here when *Shabbat* starts and won't be able to do anything until *Shabbat* is over."

I don't have time for this, Ram thought. To his father, he said, "I will sleep in Nir's apartment. It's close to the beaches and the seaside neighborhoods. I'll search for him during the day. I won't drive, only walk."

"But—"

"Abba, please, this is *pikuach nefesh*, if anything is!" Ram used *pikuach nefesh*—preservation of life—the all-encompassing trump card when it came to deciding whether one is permitted to break the *Shabbat* laws.

What he wanted to say was: *This is your son! You should be there searching for him!*

Chaim was silent for a brief moment. "Be careful, Ram."

Ram hung up and collapsed in his chair. He closed his eyes, folded his arms on the desk in front of him, and leaned his head on them, exhausted. Time to rest was a luxury he couldn't afford. The route from his army base to Tel Aviv included three long bus rides. And with public transportation ending before *Shabbat*, he would probably have to hitchhike his way south. He would try to rest on the way.

He caught a ride on the coastal highway with two female army officers who were driving south in a shiny red Fiat Punto. They dropped him off at HaYarkon Street, running parallel to the Tel Aviv beaches and the promenade. When he arrived, it was already dark. The hotels lining the shore were lit up, illuminating the shoreline. The evening was chilly, but it wasn't cold enough to keep people indoors. Millions of shining stars scattered across the clear skies.

Ram did not want to waste any time. He roamed from pubs to clubs, restaurants to twenty-four-hour kiosks, every establishment that was open on Friday night. He showed their proprietors Nir's photo. He even showed it to beggars on street corners, joggers on the promenade, dog owners on their walks. No one had seen anything.

On Saturday afternoon, exhausted and depressed, Ram reached Nir's apartment. Finding the key was easy; it was hidden inside the electric cupboard at the stair landing by the apartment. The place was empty, and the roommates were nowhere to be seen. He dropped on Nir's bed and closed his eyes. *Just for a second*, he thought.

His phone rang persistently until he heard it. He reached for it, his eyes still closed.

"Hello?"

"Ram, Officer Sela here."

Ram rose quickly. Shadows engulfed the room. The sun was too low in the skies, and the daylight outside the window almost gone. His watch told him he had slept the entire afternoon.

"What is it?" His voice was hoarse, a metallic taste in his mouth.

"I want you to meet me. Café Ness on HaYarkon Street. Do you know the place?"

"Hmm, yes, I think so."

"Good. I will be waiting for you at the entrance." Sela ended the call.

Ram rushed out and hailed a taxi. He ached for a cup of coffee, but he had no time. His head throbbed, and the unplanned deep sleep blunted his senses. In the short cab drive, he noticed he had three missing calls, two from his girlfriend Tammy and the last one from Sela. *How did I not hear these calls?* Thankful that he heard Sela's second attempt, however, he wished he had heard Tammy's voice. She would have been just what he needed to give him a moral boost.

As the driver navigated the evening traffic, night fell around them, pushing darkness into Ram's thoughts. The city, on the other hand, was waking up. Its streetlights and bars, neon signs and city buses, party-goers and night-surfers—all coming to life to illuminate *the city that never stops.*

His phone buzzed again. Millie tried to reach him, merely minutes after *Shabbat* was over. Ram ignored the call. How could he deal with her without a lead? He needed something to give them hope. Poor Millie. She must have had a terrible *Shabbat*, not knowing where Nir was, not having any way to communicate. *It will have to wait. I will call her right after I hear what Sela has to say.*

When Ram arrived at the café, Officer Sela was already sitting at a picnic table by the entrance. The patio had a collection of mismatched outdoor furniture. A dirty, though empty, ashtray stood at the edge of the tabletop.

Sela was bald, short, and muscular, his civilian clothes too tight for his bulky frame. When he saw Ram, he stood and asked, in his calm voice, "Ram?"

Ram nodded, stretching his hand. Sela shook it with rock-crushing force.

"Do you want something to drink?" Sela asked. He was holding a paper cup of steaming hot coffee.

"No, I don't have time for this. I fell asleep; too much time was wasted," Ram said.

"Wait. Just sit for a few minutes."

Ram heard the serious tone in his voice and saw the severe look in his eyes.

"Did you find something? What is it?"

Sela kept quiet. His eyes averted to a point behind Ram. Ram turned around and saw his father approaching from the other side of the street. He parked his car in a no-parking zone, something he never did. He was still wearing his *Shabbat* clothes, the white dress shirt crumpled, the dark pants creased in all the wrong places. The soles of his patent leather shoes made small pattering noises on the hard road.

They waited as Chaim crossed the street, jaywalking through the early evening traffic. A stray cat, skinny as a toothpick, traversed the road in the opposite direction.

When Chaim reached them, he shook Sela's hand.

"Mr. Levi," Sela greeted him, his expression unchanged.

Chaim nodded.

It had been three months since Ram had seen him. In the artificial light of the streetlamps, dark shadows stretched from under his brows and across his face, down to his jawline. Ram could barely see his eyes, and the skin under them drooped and sagged, like the extra skin of the stray cat, hanging sadly from its underbelly.

It struck Ram as he thought, *He looks so old.*

A tremor passed between Ram's shoulder blades and up the back of his neck. *This is what you are doing to him, you and Nir. You are the same,* the ghostly tremor seemed to whisper in his ear. Ram shook his head to rid of the momentary sensation.

"Please, let's sit down. I will tell you everything I know," Sela's voice sounded muffled.

Ram couldn't argue. He just wanted to feel normal again. He sat next to his dad, across from Sela. The picnic table bench was low and hard.

"We have found some clothes that could match your brother's, based on the description you gave me," he looked straight at Ram. "They were dumped in an alley just behind the Opera Tower, not far from the beach. We didn't find any wallet or ID."

Ram rubbed his forehead with his hand. "But it could be anybody's!"

"We took them to his roommates. They identified the clothes as the same he wore last time they saw him."

When did that happen? While he was sleeping in Nir's bed? He had not heard anything, and no one bothered to check for him. It was stupid not to have left them a note somewhere visible, to tell them he was there. How stupid can he be?

"So, what are you telling us? That it's Nir's and that he disappeared without his clothes? It could be anybody's. A homeless person or a thief who dumped them from a suitcase he stole." Ram knew he sounded desperate, yet he tried to avoid the worst-case scenario.

Sela paused for a second or two, adjusting his place on the bench. "His roommates identified them positively as the shirt, pants, and light jacket he wore that day," he repeated patiently. "We didn't find shoes. He might have put them somewhere else."

Ram glanced at his father. He was looking for a reaction. Would he accept what Sela was telling them? The expression on his father's face had not changed since he arrived.

"Here, look at this." Sela handed them his cellphone. The screen backlight was on full power, and the glow illuminated their faces from below. The photo app was open, and Ram saw the unmistakable shapes of shorts and a T-shirt on a street corner. Someone folded and stacked them neatly next to a whitewashed wall. Ram pinched the picture to zoom in. On the exposed section of the shirt, just below the neckline, he could see the top of a large letter "I" and a heart symbol to its right.

"This is how we found them," Sela said.

"NL," Ram whispered. The blood left his face and he felt light-headed.

"What did you say?" Sela asked.

"NL," Ram repeated, louder. "I heart NL."

"Yes, exactly." Sela leaned over and swiped the picture to reveal the next one. In it, the T-shirt was unfolded and spread flat on the ground.

Ram shook his head, refusing to accept what he saw. It was Nir's shirt. He couldn't deny it.

At his side, his father sighed heavily. "Ram and Millie gave Nir this shirt on his fifteenth birthday." He was talking to Sela, though Ram felt his father was talking to himself, talking about Nir for the first time after such a long time. "They bought it online from some Dutch website and got it in the mail almost a month after his birthday. He loved the pun."

"The pun?" Sela looked at it with a new curiosity, tilting the phone his way.

"NL—Nir Levi. I love Nir Levi. Millie found that NL was short for the Netherlands, and for days she searched online 'til she found a way to purchase one and had it shipped here." His mouth crooked into a little smile.

Sela's phone rang in Ram's hand. The ringtone was the opening tune for one of the TV news editions, and the caller ID identified the caller only as "Central." Sela snatched the device, and while answering the call he rose to his feet and stood to the side, his back to Ram and his father. Ram couldn't hear him nor see the expression on his face.

Chaim looked at Ram. He put his hand on Ram's, squeezing gently. The touch was cold and stiff, sending a chill up Ram's back. If his father was trying to achieve a comforting effect, he had failed miserably. Ram felt more anxious, and lonely, than before. They waited quietly for Sela to finish his call. When he did, he turned around and said, "Come."

Ram jumped to his feet. "Was that about the search? Did you find something?" He couldn't read the expression on Sela's face. His heart quickened in anticipation. *But why doesn't he say anything?*

Sela walked briskly outside of the café's patio, not waiting for them to follow. "We will take my car, it's not far from here." He led them to a beat-up Toyota. Chaim and Ram didn't bother with seat belts.

Sela drove for about ten minutes, heading north. Ram looked at his father, sitting in the passenger seat, staring straight ahead. *How can you be so calm?* Ram wanted to shout. But he held his tongue and hoped for the best.

When they reached the old Tel Aviv port, a renovated complex that boasted restaurants, bars, and high fashion stores, Sela turned left and sped over the speed bumps. He flashed his detective ID to the guard on duty, who let him through the entrance gate. He then navigated the maze of inner roads and parking lots.

Sharp police lights flickered at the road's dead end, in the passengers drop off area, where the pedestrian boardwalk started. The blue and red lights pulsed and washed the walls of a nearby one-story building, people's faces, and idle cars.

Ram's heart sank further. He had hoped to find Nir somewhere, maybe away with a friend on a road trip to Eilat or on an assignment from work. Anything but this.

In the passenger seat, his father looked straight ahead toward the cluster of flashing lights. He didn't stir.

"I don't want to alarm you," Sela brought the Toyota to a stop next to the police cars. He turned around to face them. "It might not be Nir. About an hour ago we found the body of a young man. He washed up from the sea at the edge of the promenade, on the rock barrier."

Ram shook his head violently, and his entire body shuddered. Bile forced its way up his stomach and into his throat. Breathing was difficult.

"The body's general description fits with your brother's, but we can't tell for sure. We would like to see if one of you can identify him."

Chaim still didn't say a word. He nodded his agreement.

Ram was too upset to speak coherently. He opened the door, rushed out, and stumbled to the ground, sick to his stomach, his head spinning. He had to hold the car to steady himself.

His father calmly got out of the Toyota. "Stay here, Ram," he commanded. "Sit in the car. I will go with Officer Sela."

Sela led Chaim between the police cars, the lights painting him blue, and red, and blue again. Ram followed him with his gaze. He now saw what was behind the police cars. It was a body on the ground, covered with a white sheet. Two uniformed policemen secured the area with a crime scene tape, keeping bystanders away. A small crowd had built up, bright lights flashing from cameras and mobile phones.

The entire scene was short and extremely painful. Sela stood by while a female detective pulled the sheet off the body's face. At first, Chaim just stood there. Then he collapsed to his knees, his back to Ram.

The crashing waves in the black sea below the promenade drummed in Ram's ears, growing faster and louder, penetrating deeper in his head. A single scream left his mouth. Nir was gone.

CHAPTER 1

Monday, Second Day of the Shiva

RAM

Ram sat on the low brown sofa. On a normal day, it was just the brown sofa at his father's home. The same brown sofa his parents bought when they were expecting him. The same brown sofa his mom loved so much and took care of as if it was her firstborn. The same sofa that was reserved for special guests, and the one they couldn't sit on to watch TV holding even a cup of water.

Now, it was the mourners' seat.

Used by his father, himself, and his younger sister.

Someone removed the cushions and stored them in the spare room. It used to be Nir's room, but it had been several years since he set foot in the house, so now it was just the spare room. Underneath him Ram felt the hard planks of wood that formed the structure of the bulky thing. Yellowish stains of old age dotted the fabric.

I don't remember seeing these last time, he thought.

The last time had been five years ago when his mother had passed away, and now they were sitting *shiva* again. All around him, the apartment was transformed once more, mourning with them the loss of yet another family member—his brother Nir.

Orphan nails and hooks dotted the walls; the pictures had been removed and stacked along with the sofa cushions.

The same hands rolled up the large area rugs and stored them away. The bare polished stone floor felt cold under Ram's feet; his socks were too thin. A white bed sheet covered up the large mirror on the wall across from the main door, as well as the breakfront cabinet since its rear wall was a reflective mirror. In a similar way, the silver menorahs, candlesticks, and *kiddush* cups were also hidden. *God forbid I would look at my reflection and be so vain that I forget my sorrow!* Ram might have thought along those lines had it not been for that same sorrow that stripped the rough edges off the religious cynic he had become in recent years.

The dining table was pushed all the way to the other end of the dining alcove, covered with a white tablecloth. On it lay a stack of prayer books and Psalms booklets, a cardboard box with a variety of *kippahs,* and a large white memorial candle. The label on it read, "7 Days Candle, 100% Vegetable Oil." A large glass pitcher stood next to the candle. Filled with water and untouched, the little flame danced on its shiny surface.

On the other side of the fat candle, a single picture frame stood on the table. Nir's photo. Ram liked this one—it was the last picture he took of Nir, six months ago, maybe more. He couldn't remember exactly. In it, Nir was not smiling, but rather looked to one side, unaware of the photo being taken. It was late afternoon, and they had swum at one of the last unattended strips of shore along the Mediterranean, some-where between Netanya and Haifa. After Nir had satisfied his need to fight the waves, they sat on the warm sand. They talked about their lives. They talked about missing *Imma,* their mother. They talked about work. But they didn't talk about *Abba,* their father. Ram was glad he had brought his semi-pro camera. He snapped some pictures of the waves breaking over the turquoise water, a series of images starring a family of seagulls diving to fish and then fighting over the bounty, and that one picture of Nir. He was looking into the sea, the same sea that was his best friend, but in six months' time would become his worst enemy, taking his life, taking him from them. In the picture, both subject and photographer oblivious to its future usage at the *shiva* house, the descending sun above the horizon washed Nir's face with intense orange light.

Similar sunlight now penetrated through the brown glass wall at the far end of the living room. As was done in many older-built Israeli apartments, Ram's parents removed the large case-like glass sliding doors that separated the living area from the closed-off balcony, thus enlarging the living room. They also invested in an air conditioning unit, and to keep the cool temperature inside, they installed large glass windows just in front of the green plastic shutters. The flaps on the shutters were partially open, allowing the rays of sun to come through the glass. Tiny particles of dust floated lazily in its passage into the room and onto a row of empty chairs.

Ram's father, Chaim, sat at the other end of the sofa. His face pale and long, his head full of hair—impressive for a man of fifty-five—with some strands sticking out in an uncharacteristic manner. His knitted *kippah* covered the back of his head. It was old and unwashed, and the colors had faded. Dark bags drooped under his eyes, and his stubble was already long—as if his electric shaver had been on strike for a whole week. *I don't know how his bristles don't itch!* Ram couldn't stand his own facial hair growing for more than a day or two. In the army he shaved every day, sometimes twice. *Thirty days without shaving!* He hated the prospect of what he would have to endure. When his mother had passed away, it hadn't bothered him that much because he was younger and could not grow a full beard. But more importantly, back then he still believed.

Believed in God, believed in His one true religion, and believed in the tradition and the laws. Back then he learned all the mourner's dos and don'ts, one of which forbade him from having a haircut or a shave for thirty days. Still, he shaved as soon as the month had ended. His father, on the other hand, kept his beard for a whole year after his wife's death. Ram thought it was his father's way to prolong people's pity. After all, as her husband, he wasn't obligated to mourn for longer than thirty days.

Between them sat Millie, Ram and Nir's younger sister. She gripped an open prayer book in her lap. Her back and shoulders slumped, her body curled inward like she was trying to squeeze into a smaller space. She recited prayers soundlessly, with only her mouth moving. Her eyes were closed shut, tears wet her lashes, and deep creases lined her forehead and temples. Her long hair was loosely tucked in a low ponytail. *Poor Millie. Imma died before her Bat Mitzvah, and she had never recovered completely from the loss. How could a father and two older brothers fill in for the mother she had lost?* Ram watched her grow into a shy, introverted teenager. Many times he felt guilty for neglecting her, but there were always other things to do, other places to be; his army career, running away from his own grief, and Nir.

Ram looked at the space between them. It was too roomy on the long sofa. When they sat *shiva* mourning for their mother, Nir filled that space sitting between Millie and himself, being the sandwich brother that he is.

Was. The brother that he *was.*

Ram couldn't think about Nir in the past tense. *He really is gone.* The pain was stronger than he remembered. *Imma had cancer, and she prepared us for the end. She knew we had to deal with it, be strong. But how can I deal with this?* For two days now, his heart had ached and his stomach clenched in a tight knot since that terrible moment at the old sea port, from which his mind seemed to remember only the interchanging lights—blue, and red, and blue again.

A dozen or so people sat across the sofa. They all came to console the mourners. They were mostly men but also included a few women and even a couple of children. Amongst them sat Mr. Pollack, the neighbor from the second floor.

"We haven't seen Nir for so long," Mr. Pollack said. "I bet he was busy at work. Wasn't he?" His mouth half hid behind his bushy mustache, and both thick eyebrows echoed it like a pair of mini mustaches. His eyes focused on Chaim, trying to squeeze the answer out of him.

"Uh-huh…" Chaim nodded.

"Where did he work?" Mr. Pollack continued his inquiries.

"Hmm, here and there…" Chaim whispered. His eyes were glassy. They didn't blink as he stared blankly at a spot on Mr. Pollack's nose.

"It's such a loss, such a loss…" Mr. Pollack said. "At such a young age! Not even twenty-one. And to go like this…" He shook his head from side to side.

A sharp sob burst out of Millie's mouth. For a second she opened her eyes to look at Mr. Pollack, then squeezed them shut and started swaying back and forth, holding the prayer book tighter, closer to her heart.

Ram glanced at her and then back at Mr. Pollack.

You idiot, he wanted to shout. *Can't you see how upset you made her?* But he didn't want to make a scene. He leaned to her side and put a gentle hand on her shoulder. *This will be a long week.* Ram sighed.

Chaim didn't seem to notice. "Yes… yes…" He nodded.

A hush fell over the living room as a bearded man entered through the front door. Rabbi Zechariah was the spiritual leader of Chaim's synagogue. Just the previous day, he was the one who cut Chaim and Ram's shirts just below the neckline as they started the funeral. Ram followed the back of his long black coat as they slowly walked behind the gurney to the fresh grave. Rabbi Zechariah walked with Chaim, their shoulders almost touching. Ram couldn't handle his father. Not yet.

Several people stood up in respect for the rabbi. The women, anticipating the ceremony to come, quickly gathered up the children and took them to the kitchen at the back of the apartment.

Mr. Pollack didn't notice the change around him. "Every time I saw Nir he had such a big smile on his face!" He said. "Do you know that once he helped me fix our water drain in the kitchen? He had golden hands… golden hands, I am telling you!"

Rabbi Zechariah put a hand on Mr. Pollack's shoulder. Mr. Pollack raised his head, finally noticing the presence of the rabbi in the room.

"Rabbi." Mr. Pollack stood and moved to the side.

Rabbi Zechariah approached the mourners, nodded his head lightly, and said, "*Baruch Dayan Emet.*"

Some of the men around the room murmured, repeating the phrase: *Blessed He who judges true.*

Ram nudged his sister gently on her elbow. "Go, Millie. Join the women in the kitchen."

Millie opened her eyes, stopped chanting, and stared at him. *How can you send me away?* her stare seemed to say. She clung to his side and slumped deeper into the cushionless sofa.

When she saw that everyone was staring at her, waiting for her, she quickly got up and ran to the kitchen. Ram's heart ached for her. However, this was what tradition dictated, and following her with his gaze, he saw her shoulders straighten in resolution as she turned around, just behind the last row of men, preparing herself for the service.

"It's *Mincha* time," Rabbi Zechariah said.

The men stood and positioned themselves toward the east. Most of them had *kippahs* on their heads, either wearing them on a regular basis or carrying them in their back pockets for such occasions. The rest took one from the box on the dining table and covered their heads. They used the prayer books borrowed from the central synagogue or recited the prayers by heart. Two men pulled out their smartphones, launched a prayer app, and used high-tech media for the thousand-year-old ritual.

"Rabbi, *bechavod*, will you lead us in the service?" Chaim said.

"No," Rabbi Zechariah shook his head. "You or Ram should be our *chazan*. You have to recite the *Kaddish*."

Chaim closed his eyes and rubbed his scruff chin with his hand. When he opened his eyes, he looked at Ram and nodded to him, pointing his chin toward the front of the room.

Ram understood the request, but still hesitated. He knew what needed to be done. He wasn't shy nor did he have stage fright. During his years in the *yeshiva*, he sometimes led the service even though he hadn't the best voice nor the zealotry that some of his classmates possessed for everything religious. And when his mother passed away, he had performed the same tradition with passion and care, believing he helped raise his mom's *neshamah*, her spirit, to the heavens.

But now it was different. *Everything was different.*

Ram slowly got up to his feet, turned in the same direction as the rest of the men, and recited, "*Ashrey yoshvei betecha od yehalelucha selah.*" *Happy are those who dwell in Your house; may they always praise you.* Rabbi Zechariah picked up a *tallit* bag, took the prayer shawl out, and gently wrapped it around Ram's slender shoulders.

After the prayers were over, the men settled down, finding empty seats amongst the many folded chairs brought in for the week. It was almost time for *Ma'ariv,* the evening's service, and traditionally the mourners and their visitors learned some chapters from the *Mishnah* to fill the time.

Millie was still with the women, so Chaim patted the space next to him on the sofa when Ram approached. "Come, Ram. Sit next to me," he said, though his eyes avoided Ram's, looking instead at space on the cold stone floor in front of him.

Ram obeyed his father's request and sat down, his body reflexively trying to keep some distance between them.

While Rabbi Zechariah read and explained the meaning of the chapter he chose to study, more people arrived, filling up the already stuffy room. Someone passed a clipboard around with a couple of sheets of paper, listing the entire *Mishnah*'s tractates. At the top of the first page, bold black letters read: **Learn in memory of Nir, son of Chaim Levi. May his memory be a blessing**. Some of the younger men wrote their names next to the portion they volunteered to learn in the next thirty days. Ram saw that most of the list was still empty. *Good luck with filling this up,* he thought. For his mother, when she passed away, he took it on himself and spent days and nights learning, praying for the ascending of her soul into higher spheres. Now he couldn't, *wouldn't,* do it again.

When his mother was alive, life was simpler and so much happier. Ram's best memories were from special days like *Shabbat* and holidays, when everything seemed brighter, smelled sweeter, and felt special. Every Friday night after lighting the candles, one for each family member, his mother's face shone brightly. Dishes of fish, *bourekas*, and quiches filled with vegetables and cheese kept warm on the hot plate, their aromas filling the house, the feast she prepared waited for their return from *beit haknesset*. The children wore their *Shabbat* clothes, Ram and Nir with white shirts and blue or khaki pants, Millie in dresses—bright colors in the summer, dark velvet or knitted wool in the colder months of the year. Millie loved walking with them to the synagogue, going up to the women's section and peeking down at them through the white curtain dividers. When she grew impatient, she would come down into the men's section. She was still young enough for this to be acceptable. Ram remembered fondly how she would find the old candy-man who gave her a soft toffee, and then she would sit on their father's lap until it was time to go home. She would skip ahead in front of them, running along the white divider line in the middle of the road while they strolled behind, claiming the street to themselves like the rest of the city's pedestrians. Ram had always walked alongside their father, and Nir followed behind.

On special holidays his mother would join them, but on Friday nights she liked staying behind, relaxing on her sofa after a busy day of cleaning the house and preparing food for the *Shabbat* meals. When they reached home, his mother always smiled, light in her eyes. She sang their names and kissed them on their cheeks, one by one. Everyone had their favorite dish, and she always made something for each, making them all feel special. Ram's favorite was the sole fish, on which he smeared tahini and squeezed lemon juice. Nir loved her stuffed gefilte fish. He always asked her to buy a live carp, just like their grandmother used to. When they visited *Savta* before the High Holidays, she usually had a fat fish swimming in the bathtub for a few days. What they never saw was how *Savta* killed it with two strong blows to its head. Then she would gut it, clean it inside out, and divide it into portions for filling and cooking. "No way!" Imma used to say, wrinkling her nose, "I am not going to kill the fish and clean it! I am more than happy to pay someone else to do it. My mother grew up like this in Poland. Thank God she doesn't grow her own chicken in her little apartment. Can you imagine that!" She would then cluck like a hen, make a funny face, and burst out laughing, and that was the end of it.

A thin smile crept onto Ram's face, while a soft but steady pressure built behind his eyes. He pushed on them hard with the back of his hands, as if he could squeeze the memories, and the agony they always brought, back in. Put them in check until the next time they resurface. When he finally removed his hands and opened his eyes, he blinked repeatedly, focusing his vision on the room. Rabbi Zechariah was silent. He completed the short study and looked at Ram, expectantly.

What happened? Ram couldn't comprehend why Rabbi Zechariah was in the house, his face so somber. And all these men around him, united in their heavy expressions, tired eyelids hooding over dark pupils, all looking at him. And then it came back to him.

Nir was dead.

Dead.

"*Ma'ariv.*" The one word in his father's voice brought him back. Ram stood again to lead the night service. This time, he didn't hesitate. He was on autopilot, the old habits coming back. The words he thought he had put behind him came back immediately as if he still said them every day. The familiar verses, the rhythm of the prayer—they brought with them an unexpected warm feeling, deep in his stomach, a small safe haven in the chaos of the last few days. He closed his eyes, reciting the blessings by heart.

When they were kids, Nir admired Ram's ability to remember all the prayers' words. They used to sit next to their father in the large synagogue while their friends played in the yard at the front of the building. Ram always stood at the right times, and during the High Holidays he sometimes stood throughout the entire *tefilah*. Nir followed his direction, wanting to be more like him, hoping their father would look at him in the same way, with pride and admiration.

Ram closed the service, stepping three steps backward, bowing to each side of the room, completing the *Kaddish*. The crowded room swayed behind him. Men shuffled their feet, folded some of the chairs, collected the prayer books, and rearranged the room for the remainder of the night. The men who came only for the service and wished to leave formed a line in front of the grieving family members. Ram dropped in next to his father, his hands loose in his lap. He just wanted this all to be over with.

One by one, each of the consoling men stood in front of Chaim and Ram, saying, "*Hamakom yenachem etchem betoch shea'r aveley tzion ve'Yerushalaim*"; *May He comfort you among the other mourners of Zion and Jerusalem*. Rabbi Zechariah sat in the chair adjacent to the mourners' sofa, waiting patiently for the crowds to dwindle so he could pay his respects. Chaim and Ram just nodded their heads, saying nothing, shaking no hands.

Ram was familiar with most of the faces. Mr. Pollack had come with his son and two grandsons. Shalom Rott, the synagogue's *gabbay*, who managed the day-to-day logistics of the congregation, came accompanied by his entourage of young high school helpers. There were more; many of the neighborhood's men and their sons, sons-in-law, brothers. Others in line were strangers; men who needed a quick place to pray the evening services; men who took on themselves to fulfill the *mitzvah* of consoling the bereaved, who went out of their way to find *shiva* houses and join the *minyan*; men who looked for the black-and-white obituary announcements around the city and wanted to see whose life had just gotten worse, who was the family behind the name, what could be learned about them. Ram could sense it in their eyes, the way they looked at him and his father, assessing them, trying to read into their souls. As disgusted as they made him feel, he succumbed to the process.

Just let it go, he kept telling himself.

The next man in line was thin, of average height, and in his late thirties. He had short trimmed hair and a beard. He wore a simple white T-shirt and blue jeans, with a crumpled *kippah* on his head. He didn't stand out even though many of the other men were wearing button-down white shirts with black or dark blue slacks. Still, the crowd was a mix of modern and traditional attire—working men and *yeshiva* students, some soldiers in uniforms, and even a physician in his scrubs.

When it was the man's turn to say his departing words, he just stood there. He looked down at Ram and his father as they sat on the low sofa. No one made a sound. Chaim looked at the stranger, waiting for him to be the first to say something. Ram thought he might help him. Visiting a *shiva* house can be daunting for many, not knowing what to say, not knowing all the rules and traditions of bereavement. But he was not supposed to get up to greet people, nor to escort them to the door.

To Ram's surprise, his father stood up, his eyes at the same level as the stranger.

"Don't," said the man.

The stranger stretched his hand and touched Chaim's arm, resting his fingers on it. His other hand gently held Chaim's hand in place, engulfing the fingers into a fist. His eyes locked with Chaim's. They stood frozen, unmoving. For a split second, Ram sensed the slightest tremor in his father's face, an undercurrent weaving its way from the center, right between his eyes, pushing and smoothing the skin outward—up to the roots of his hair, sideways, to the base of his ears, and down his cheeks through the rough expanse of facial hair.

The change in his father's expression was quick yet profound. Ram was drawn into Chaim's brown irises. They grew wide as his pupils shrank into two black dots.

Later he would berate himself for being so irresponsible. But, at that moment, Ram didn't react to the stranger, only to his father. The stranger turned around to leave. He quietly made his way through the line of men behind him while they forced themselves closer to the mourners' sofa. In a second or two, he completely disappeared behind their shoulders, as if space there sucked him through.

Chaim stood at the same position, his arm slightly raised, the fingers still closed in a tight fist, suspended in the air as if the man was still holding it in his grip.

"Abba?" Ram said. "Are you okay?"

Chaim ignored him. His face turned white, as white as the bedsheet thrown on the wall mirror. Tears pooled under his eyes.

"Abba? What's wrong?" Ram raised his hand to touch Chaim's arm. The skin was so hot that his fingers burned to the touch. At the same instant, Chaim's knees buckled under him, and he dropped heavily on the floor.

CHAPTER 2

CHAIM

I stand on a beach. The wind blows behind me, ruffling my hair and the tail of my shirt.

Where am I? How did I get here?

The air is cold. The wind changes direction, and it sprays sand and water in my face. I can taste the salt on my tongue. Sand particles find their way into my ears, down my clothes, through the collar of my shirt, and under the layers of *tzitzit* and sleeveless undershirt. My shoes become heavy and uncomfortable as they, too, fill quickly with the beige substance. I raise one hand to shield my eyes. For the briefest moment, my mind registers that my other hand is holding a hard object, small and smooth. And warm. The wind, however, is too strong, and I am busy protecting myself from its wrath.

The sky has turned a sickly orange tint. The ocean breaks ahead of me with crashing waves, one following the other so rapidly that the sea cannot rest in between. I sense movement around me—crabs scurrying around, looking for mates and food. Loner seagulls dive, trying to fish one last meal before nightfall.

There is more. Larger than the crabs and the seagulls. A human, right there on the beach.

Nir.

But how can it be?

Nir is *here*, right there in front of me!

His back is toward me, but I recognize him and would do so even if the beach had been crowded like on the hottest summer day. Now the strip of land is deserted. Nir and I are the only people here.

My son crouches on the sand where the water reaches the shore. He looks so skinny, his shoulders hunched, his hair too long for my liking. Nir never liked to listen, even about the little things. And this stupid Dutch T-shirt! He loved it and wore it to threads. I see the holes in the back, his skin exposed, as pale as the bleached fabric. I also recognize his Bermuda shorts. Sarah bought them for him.

My heart misses a beat.

Using his bare hands, Nir plays in the sand. Breaking the surface of the wet sand, he picks mud from a small round trench and piles it in the middle of the circle. He lets the water drip on the pile, the mud forming a magical mountain, a black mound of tiny stalagmites. The wind, water, and sand don't seem to bother him. His focus is on the sand and the magical little mountain.

"Nir," I call him.

I move forward, thinking the wind will help me, push me toward him. Instead, I must push with all my might against a power as intense as an army tank—fighting, shoving me, not allowing me to get any closer.

Nir doesn't hear me. He continues playing in the sand.

"Nir! Nir, answer me!" I cry. His back is stubbornly facing me, the white T-shirt stretched on his body. The waves keep crashing forcefully, the sea pushing itself onshore with every new foamy arch.

"Nir, be careful! Stay away from the water!"

He keeps sitting there, his hands digging deeper and deeper, the crashing waves nearly touching his feet.

A dark dread fills me from within. I have to get him away from the water, as far as possible, where it's dry and safe. Away from this hateful sea. Day after day it pretends to be your ally, treacherously making you trust it so you allow your loved ones into its wet arms, and then, on one normal afternoon, it takes your son away from you.

I push harder, feeling my strength draining quickly. I make some progress, though it's slow and the tide rises quickly, faster than me. The sea seems to laugh at me and say, *Here I come to take him again, and there is nothing you can do.* I won't let it win again, so I move forward. When I finally reach the distance and I think I can reach my hands to hold onto Nir's shoulders, force him to turn around and look at me, to acknowledge me, to make him come with me, I freeze in place. The wind stops. The water calms down and nearly cease its constant race to the shore. The last seagull flies away, and the crabs hide in their underground burrows. The dread inside me intensifies, as if my intestines have solidified into lead, and my heart is pumping mercury throughout my veins. Something bad is going to happen. I can feel it with every remaining cell of my body that had not yet turned into cold dark metal.

"Nir," my voice sounds harsh and loud, unadjusted to the sudden quiet that has fallen around us. I swallow, and bits of sand slide slowly down my throat. I try again to grab Nir's attention, this time in a lower, hushed voice, "Nir, please. It's Abba."

Nir stops digging. He breathes steadily, and his hunched shoulders rise slightly with every inhale. I can faintly smell a familiar scent of sweat and white glue. Nir's. I want to reach him so badly, to talk to him, to warn him, and take him away from the wet monster lurking nearby. Did his head just drop slightly? Was he listening?

Suddenly Nir's body twitches. He gets to his feet, leaning forward, retching. I want to help him, but I can't move. He coughs several times, his body folding forward, his hands on his knees, his head between his legs. Water pours out of his mouth. Green slimy water. It hits the sand below him, splashing little droplets onto his ankles. *He is drowning!* The words bounce frantically in my head, hitting my skull from within. Before I can even try to do something—unfreeze, move toward him, anything—it stops. He straightens up and stands in place, still and soundless.

In the quiet air, in this sudden vacuum, time stretches like elastic dough. I notice his entirety. Sand covers the crown of his head like a misshapen *kippah*, ears hiding behind the mound of brown hair. His shoulder blades poke hard into the stretched fabric of his shirt. The dampness at the bottom of his pants. The little patches of hair that started sprouting on his skinny legs. The old sneakers on his feet. No socks. He is not wearing any socks.

Then he turns around.

CHAPTER 3

Monday, Second Day of the Shiva

RAM

"Abba!" Ram kneeled down on the floor next to his father. Behind him, a ring of men threatened to suffocate both of them. "Wake up, Abba!" In his panic, his inner boy wanted to shake his father's shoulder, slap his father's face, do something to wake him up. During his army service, he had been trained in first aid and emergency situations, but now he couldn't remember what needed to be done first. Could he move his father's head? Should he start CPR?

Don't panic, the soldier inside him said. *He needs air. We need a doctor. He will be fine!*

The room was still crowded with the remaining men waiting to give their condolences and several who sat down to stay longer. As if reading his thoughts, several voices from the crowd shouted:

"Doctor! We need a doctor!"

"Is anyone here a physician? A medic or a nurse? Someone?"

"Call one-zero-one, quick!"

Dr. Frisch, a young man in sky-blue scrubs, pushed his way through the human ring. At the same time, *gabbay* Rott took control of the situation. He asked people to leave and clear the room, allowing for space and air around Ram and his father. Dr. Frisch kneeled next to Ram and gently pushed him aside, making space to help Chaim. With one hand he tilted Chaim's head backward, while the other hand pulled Chaim's chin upward. Chaim's mouth opened, and Dr. Frisch leaned down to listen, his ear almost touching Chaim's face. Dr. Frisch's eyes searched intently for breathing movement on Chaim's chest.

"Good. He is breathing," he confirmed.

Ram exhaled too, releasing some of the tension in his mind.

Dr. Frisch continued with a rapid examination, first checking Chaim's pulse, followed by opening Chaim's eyes to look into his pupils. A nod and a smile followed every positive reaction he observed.

Chaim's face was ashen pale and shone with sweat. Suddenly, as unexpectedly as his fall, his eyes opened, and his body jerked upward. He raised his head off the floor and tried to lean on his elbows, pushing himself into a sitting position.

"Relax, Mr. Levi. You fainted," Dr. Frisch said. With strong hands, he pushed on Chaim's shoulder, steadying him back to lie on the floor. "Your vitals are not too bad, your pulse is a bit too fast, and you are very pale. Do you feel any pain?"

Chaim, visibly confused, shook his head.

"Okay, that's good. Are you drinking enough water? Ram?" He looked at Ram, his eyes peeking over the rim of his metal glasses.

"He does, I think." Ram hadn't paid much attention to his father's water intake.

"The house is too crowded and stuffy," Dr. Frisch continued. "Everyone should leave now and allow Mr. Levi to rest."

With *gabbay* Rott's supervision, some of the men had already left. Seeing now that things were under control, the remaining ones nodded in consent. As they turned around to leave, Millie ran from the kitchen, accompanied by Chava, their aunt, Chaim's older sister.

"Abba!" Millie said. "What happened?"

Chava stood next to her, looking at Chaim perched on the floor. Her hands covered her mouth, stifling whatever might come out.

Chaim looked around the room, his head moving sharply from side to side, his eyes wide open.

"Abba, what's wrong?" Ram asked.

"Nir—the beach, a seagull. Nir—it was Nir!"

"Nir? Where?" Ram fought the urge to look over his shoulders, but of course, Nir was not there. What was his father talking about? "You are not making any sense, Abba."

"I believe your father is in shock," Dr. Frisch said. "He must get some rest. He should go to the ER to do some tests." They heard a siren in the distance getting closer.

"No!" Chaim shouted.

Ram and Dr. Frisch turned their heads in unison toward Chaim.

"But you—" Dr. Frisch started.

"Abba—" Ram said.

"No need for the hospital," Chaim said in a calmer, decisive voice. "I feel," he gasped slowly, "much better now."

"I don't like this," Dr. Frisch shook his head slowly.

"I will be fine," Chaim said, putting his hand on Dr. Frisch's arm. "I promise. Just help me get to bed. I will rest and drink plenty of water. Everything will be fine."

Dr. Frisch still looked doubtful. Eventually, he raised his hands. "Okay, no hospital for you this time. But you must rest, and I will come by tomorrow morning to check on you, maybe even bring a kit to take your blood for some tests. Ram, come. Help me."

They helped Chaim to his feet, positioned him gently between them, his arms anchored to their shoulders, and slowly walked him to his room. Millie followed them with a glass of water for their father. They gently helped Chaim onto his bed. Dr. Frisch signaled Ram to come back with him to the living room.

Chava waited for them outside the bedroom's door. "The ambulance from Magen David is here," she said.

Dr. Frisch sighed. "I will talk with them. Chaim doesn't want to go to the hospital, and we can't make him." He pushed through behind her, so she followed him and Ram through the narrow corridor into the living area. Before leaving, Dr. Frisch turned around to talk to them. "I believe Chaim went through some kind of shock. If he is under too much stress, I don't know how he will be able to complete the *shiva*. He might have to be admitted if he doesn't get some rest and lots of fluids in him."

"I will take care of him, Doctor, and Millie is here to help me," Ram said.

"You are not supposed to do that while sitting *shiva* for your brother, Ram." It was Rabbi Zechariah, who, Ram realized, was still hanging around. "Don't worry. I will arrange for someone to take care of him. You stay here. Everything will be fine."

"Yes, and I am here too!" Chava chimed in. "And I can ask Asher Shalom to help too."

That's the last thing I need, Ram thought. Asher Shalom was Chava's husband, which was his only saving grace. Secretly, Ram despised the man. Asher Shalom always examined how other people observed the law, and he always had criticism—this person is always late to the morning service… that woman wears her skirts a bit too short…

Yet, for his own practice, Asher Shalom would find permissions to twist the rules and fit them to his needs. *What a hypocrite!* Thinking about it, Ram realized he had not seen Asher Shalom since the funeral. He probably had found a reason to stay away. He wasn't much for helping other people in need.

Why am I even bothering with him? Ram scolded himself and tried to relax, sitting on the low seat of the sofa. *Yes, things will be okay. I have to take care of Millie and Abba, but people are here to help us. We are not alone.*

He looked around, trying to remember what had happened just before his father collapsed; the line of men consoling them, his father attempting to speak with a man he didn't recognize, and no recognition on Chaim's face when he saw the man. Ram scanned the room, but most of the visitors had already left. The room was quiet now. His aunt collected the prayer books and stacked them in a neat pile on the dining table. Then she started folding the chairs and stacked them against one of the walls.

As she worked through the room, Chava asked Ram, "Would you like something to drink? Maybe a cup of coffee? I can bring you something to eat too."

Ram shook his head. "There was a man. He talked with Abba just before Abba fainted…"

"I didn't see. I was in the kitchen," Chava said, briefly pausing to look at him. "But maybe he was here before? There were so many people, I didn't recognize most of them. What did he look like?"

"I don't know—ordinary, not religious. At least, I don't think he is. He had a beard, a short trimmed one, I am sure about that. Maybe he had a tattoo, but it could be a birthmark, on his right arm." Seeing a tattoo in this city was very uncommon, and it would have stuck out as unusual and made the man memorable, so it must have been a birthmark.

"I didn't see anyone like that. Why are you looking for him?"

"He was right there when Abba fainted. I don't know what exactly happened, but I want to speak with him and find out."

"Why don't you ask Chaim, after he rests and feels better?"

"I will…" His stomach churned at the thought. "But I still want to talk to that man!" He added impatiently.

"Well," Chava said, "maybe he will show up again tomorrow. Most of them do." With efficient movements, she continued folding the chairs, pulling them to the growing stack by the wall. "It's going to be very busy. Don't wear yourself out too much. You need your energy. This is not an easy time. When your Imma died…" Her voice trailed off. She stopped in her tracks, her gaze wandering around, moisture filling her eyes. She hurried with the last chair in hand, left it against the wall, and rushed to the back of the apartment. From behind, Ram saw her hand reaching into her pocket, searching for a crumpled tissue, her head bowed low.

CHAPTER 4

CHAIM

The little object lies on the side table between the plastic bottles and boxes of medicine. At first I think it is light reflected on the tabletop, broken and distorted by the clutter. As my eyes focus, I see there is more to it than light. Something rests there. I fumble around, my hand heavy, craning around so slowly. Bottles fly off the table and land silently onto the thick carpet. Finally, my stiff fingers close in on the little object. It is cold, and I recoil for an instant, confusing the biting-chill with a flaming-heat. I carefully touch it again with the pads of my fingertips. They caress the smooth surface, feeling for any imperfections, indents, crevices, or rough edges. There it is, one sharp edge. Not sharp enough for cutting, but otherwise a square-angled tiny ledge. My hand registers it immediately, where I knew the edge would be. My fingers know right away what my brain refuses to accept.

This is the stone that Nir gave me years ago.

He was five at the time. I remember he still couldn't read. We were at the synagogue for *Shabbat* morning service. I allowed him to play with the other boys, not before he recited with me the basics of prayers—*Mode Ani* and *Shema Yisrael*. I didn't mind letting him go with his friends. After all, he was just a boy, going into elementary school. The next year I would be stricter with him.

I dropped the little stone in the cubby below the prayer lectern and forgot about it. In the cubby I stored prayer books, my *tallit* bag, and the religious *Shabbat* newsletters. Then I found it again sometime after Nir left home to live who knows where and work at one of his odd jobs. During a daily service I searched for something in the cubby, and my hand ran upon this little intruder. I fished it up, and the memory emerged as surprising as the stone itself. Nir's face, skinny and young, missing two front teeth, his hair tousled and his white shirt untucked.

"Abba, keep this for me. Okay?" He gave me the stone, his hand clammy and covered with a thin layer of dirt.

I scolded him. Of course I did. For messing up his *Shabbat* clothes, for playing in the dirt, and for picking stones on the holy *Shabbat*. I must have told him to drop it in the cubby.

I am not a sentimental person. But years later, when Ram left home to the *Hesder Yeshiva* and later to the army, I wanted to have a memento to remind me of him when he was away. At the back of a shelf in his room, discarded on top of some books, I found a small Siddur which Ram received for his *Bar Mitzvah*. So I carried it with me, always, in one of my pockets. I was somehow embarrassed for this need, to hold on to a possession of his. After all, he was an hour drive away, we could talk on the phone almost at any time, and he came home every other weekend. So I didn't mention it to anyone, not even Sarah.

And then, when Nir left home, I had none of the same urge to carry something of his. But when I found that little pebble and the memory rose in me, I put it in my pocket and have carried it ever since.

My right hand fingers knew it by heart. They fondled it daily; on weekdays of course, not on the *Shabbat*. Like a talisman, it traveled with me from one slacks' pocket to another, and during the winters, to the warmth of a deep padded jacket pocket. Even when Nir ran away, I still kept the stone, a constant reminder of him. At times I felt like it had a twin sister stuck heavily in my throat, other times in my gut. But as constant and as disturbing, I didn't let it go.

In the haze of the last days, since we found his body on the beach, the little stone held a new meaning for me. At first, I held it in my hand like it was part of him, the only part I could keep, that no one would take from me. Then, I knew I couldn't hold on to it; it belongs with him. I decided to put it on Nir's grave. It would be my stone, the one I would place on his burial site. It would not fade and burn in the sun nor wash away in the rain.

When we headed the procession to the open gravesite, I was surrounded by men. Rabbi Zecharia walked beside me, and his presence, and the presence of the other men, tall and silent, somber and dark, engulfed me. If not for that little pebble, I would have been suffocated in their communal embrace. My hand was buried deep in my right pocket, holding the stone tightly; it has kept me company in the car on our way to the cemetery, each one of us silently observing the passing views. Then, through the gate of the cemetery, as I went with Ram into the *taharah* room to say our last goodbyes, those agonizing minutes that felt like eternity when the *chevra kadisha* unveiled Nir's face for us, and we stood beside him, each in his own contemplation, saying his own silent words. As we emerged out via the narrow door leading to the gravel lane, the short Cypresses that lined it on both sides, the white and yellowish headstones standing in row after row, the smell of dust and turned earth.

The little stone was warm in my hand, part of me by that time. It was hard to give it away, but it was the right thing to do. I held it tight as Ram and I said the *kaddish* and didn't let it out of my hand when the *chevra kadisha* quickly slid the gray slabs of cement over the shroud covered body, and then with experienced measured movements shoveled the dirt back into the hole.

I did not cry. My eyes were dry like that stone. People must have wondered, *How does he do it? Why doesn't he cry? Is he that strong?* I knew I was allowed to cry. I knew no one would judge me for crying, falling apart at my own son's funeral. What they didn't know was that my heart bled, and my hand surrounding the stone cried, pouring tears and life back into this little token of my son. My beloved lost son.

When the burial was done, I put the little stone on the fresh grave.

And now, in the darkness of my room, the little stone appears on the night table; I hold it in my hand.

How did it get here?

I squeeze it tight, now warm to the touch, as if it was held close to the body for a long time. My heartbeat quickens, and the room around me swells at the edges. Voices from behind the closed door are muffled, as if the entire room has been submerged by the sea. I rest my head on the pillow and close my eyes.

Instead of blessed darkness, I see light, and the sea is right there, without the protection of the walls of my room. I am standing on the beach again.

I open my eyes sharply. The little stone pulsates in my hand like a small heart. It is hot like a lava rock; I feel it as it simmers and boils within my tight fist. My hand opens and recoils, dropping the stone in my lap, on top of the blanket. The darkness of my room swallows me again. It is quiet, the voices from the living room had ceased. My heart thumps in my throat. Sweat runs and drenches my pajama shirt.

Chills run through my spine, and I shake uncontrollably. I pull the blanket over my shoulders, wrapping it close to my body. I doze off.

When I wake up again, the sun is already up. It must be nine or ten. I usually wake up at first light, with the trucks that deliver bread and milk to the neighborhood grocer. I am not familiar with the angle of the window above my bed in the mid-morning light.

Then I remember. Nir is dead. The fresh grave. The *shiva* house. Men in the house, so many of them. I fell. And then I was at the sea. And Nir...

Without thinking, I snap the stone from its resting place. I hold it with both hands, feeling it in my palms. I close my eyes.

***

Nir turns around and looks at me. The beach stretches long behind his back, and the sea whispers lightly by our side, but all I can see are his eyes. Sad eyes. Deep and brown and dark like the burrow holes of beach crabs. He doesn't blink. He just looks at me with those heartbroken, heartbreaking eyes.

I can't stare into his eyes for too long. If I do, I will become a pillar of salt. I must avert my gaze. His face is white and smooth like marble. Some greenish seaweed-like strands are stuck to his shoulder, tangled in his hair. Wet sand covers his knees and shins. A gash runs the length of his right shin, deep enough to see his bone and wide enough to fit two fingers. It is crimson, but no blood spills out. Something sticks out of it, but I can't make out what it is.

He starts walking toward me. The distance is short, but he doesn't seem to advance, as if he is walking in place or in space. Yet, I see him moving. Eventually, he does reach me. He doesn't acknowledge me or say a thing. He passes me.

"Nir!" I turn around on my heels to face his back. He walks, and although he has not changed his pace, he reaches farther distance with every step he takes.

"Nir, stop!"

I follow him. At first, he walks along the beach, where the sand is deep and dry. My feet sink in, grainy sand filling my shoes. Then Nir turns sharply inland where the sand becomes dirt, packed and hard. It is easier to walk on, so I hasten my pace, trying to reach him. The ground gently slopes upward, knee-high grass covers it. Nir hikes through a narrow path, zigzagging in the wavy growth.

I beg him to stop, but he ignores my calls.

The sky has changed as well, now pink, red, and orange, colored by the setting sun. I labor to keep my stride, not to lose sight of him. I am panting by the time I reach the peak of the hill. Beyond, I should see the city, large and dark, its lights slowly waking for the night. Instead all I see is more grass, with single trees speckling the view here and there. Nir is ahead of me, walking, striding, running away. Though I can still see him clearly, the gap between us grows steadily. I cannot stop to rest, lest I lose him.

About a kilometer ahead, I see a lone building in the distance. I am unsure of what it is exactly; its outline suggests a massive structure with a flat roof. Nir heads in that direction, and I follow him. The high grass rustles in the wind.

As we get closer, the ground grows barer and drier, with patches of dry yellow thistles dotting the surrounding fields. The closer we are to the building, the larger these patches are. The path widens, and I don't brush against the growth anymore.

From the corner of my eyes, I notice movement in the bushes. A gray crab hurries across one of the clearings. Its shell is shiny and reflects red and purple, its beady little eyes point both ways.

It looks at me and sees me. It will change course and come to bite me.

The thought is ridiculous! Even here—

But where is *here*? The little stone pulses lightly in my hand

—even here I know it. As if it hears my thoughts, the crab continues to the other side of the clearing, disappearing between two dry stalks. It's strange to see such a creature so far from the shore.

It doesn't matter! I have to reach Nir. I need to talk to him.

But why? How would it help now? Can I—

No, that is impossible.

The little stone pulse grows more intense, like a small beating heart in my hand.

Is it possible, though? Can I—and the thought forms in my head, and it rings true—save him? It is not a question anymore, but a statement.

I. Can. Save. Nir.

I can save him.

I look ahead of me, starting again to call for my son to stop and wait. The building is still there, featureless in the looming twilight. But Nir has disappeared.

I panic. "Ni-rrr!" his name half stuck in my throat, half blurted out. I stagger on the path and steady myself, momentarily disoriented. I must push on. No matter how tired I feel, I must continue, reach Nir, and save him.

I stop in my tracks; two crabs appear from the same direction as the first one. They hurry on their tiny legs, sprinting to follow their mate. Then more. Bigger fat black crabs. Small red ones. In groups and lone ones. I notice some with tails, raised high above their backs. Scorpions. Black and shiny, like tar. Yellow as a sick man's mucus. I keep my distance, noticing they all follow the same path as the first crab, waiting to see if they will just pass and let me through. Nir walked by here not seconds ago. I can see where his steps disturbed the dirt.

I call him. "Nir, wait… Wait! I can't see you. Stay where you are. Nir!" I don't know if he hears me. The building, from where I stand, looks larger, familiar, but I still can't place it. I hope Nir is waiting for me ahead.

The crabs are replaced by rows of scorpions, followed by snakes. Small snakes and long snakes. Black and red snakes. Yellow with white scales and green with brown and red diamonds. I back up, moving to a distance where I feel safe.

So many of the creatures pass through. The sun should be deep in the water by now. But the skies are still painted and warm. Once the path is clear, I can proceed. I move my feet and, as if by the same cue, night rushes in. The ground is black, the structure ahead of me sits heavily in the dark. An orange-tinted moon switches on, low in the horizon. The man on its surface is slightly off, a puzzled look on its ancient face.

I finally reach the building. I wish I had some way to illuminate the darkness and see where I am. I start singing in a low whisper, my voice shaking, a Hanukkah song we used to sing with the kids when they were little. *"Banu choshech legaresh… Beyadeinu or va'esh…"* We came to banish the darkness… In our hands light and fire…

Nir waits for me on the steps of the building. I can hardly see him, but I sense his presence. I don't hear breathing, not even the faintest. I just know he is here.

Still, I ask, "Nir, are you there?"

A soft yellow light floods the steps, its source hidden above us. Finally I see where I am. The Old Ashlag synagogue, the one where my father took me to as a kid, the one I took Ram and Nir to when they were young. *But why here? In the middle of these peculiar fields, so close to the sea?*

The original Old Ashlag synagogue, or as we called it, Ashlag for short, was built in the mid-nineteen-thirties and is in the heart of Bnei Brak, on the main street. By the time Nir was five, its front facade was dark gray from the pollution of passing vehicles, its pink marble an unrecognizable mix of brown and black, covered with centuries of grime and remnants of posters and signs that were glued to it: *Pashkevilles* of doom-saying rabbis warning about the *yetzer ha'rah*, the evil inclination in everything modern. Obituaries announcing the passing of prince and pauper alike. Announcements of hundreds of *gmach* organizations, offering the poor and needy everything from electric heaters for the cold winter months to wedding dresses for *Hachnasat Kallah*—helping poor young women get married with respect and dignity.

Inside, Ashlag was not much better. Funds from charity and city hall barely kept it running. The decorated high ceilings with paintings of fierce animals—a lion, a deer, an eagle—representing different traits of God, were peeling in places. The floor was worn, the wooden benches sagging, their paint long gone. The once exquisite arc, covered with inlaid multicolor marble design and featuring a pleasant curtain, was run down. Too many years of daily usage, strangers who came and went, not enough money to keep its old glory.

Nir stands on the top stair. He is facing the massive doors, his back still to me. When I reach him, before I have the chance to stop him, to put my hand on his shoulder and make him turn around and face me, he pulls on the long brass handle and effortlessly opens the wing door.

Beyond the gaping door, the synagogue interior is dark and uninviting. Nir steps in, and I trail behind. The light follows us, an unnatural glow that seems to come from nowhere. When we are inside, the door quietly closes behind us. The place is deserted, yet I can't remember ever seeing it empty. Prayer books are scattered on the lecterns, waiting for the next service, for the next worshippers to pick them up. Most of them are worn, the gold embossed letters on their covers long gone, the pages yellow, thin, and parchment-like in the most used sections. The ornamental curtain covering the front of the holy ark is dark red, like a dry pool of blood, and the thick threads of the stitched twin lions decoration are unravelling at places. Looking up at the painted ceiling, the animals look at each other in an eternal, infinite loop—a crab, a scorpion, a snake. Were these the original animals? No. I shake my head, blinking. They are still there. A red crab. A yellow scorpion. A black snake. But what were the original paintings? Suddenly, I can't remember.

Below them, around half of the perimeter of the building hang the lace curtains that cover the women's balcony. They gently flutter as if women stand behind them, their small hands poking at the cloth, their prayers mute, dry air blowing from their mouths only to be stopped by the thin fabric. Maybe a window is open at the back of the balcony. That must be it.

Nir approaches the back of the men's section, directly under the women's balcony. The ceiling there is lower, making it a bit cozier. He sits down on a bench, a book open in front of him. He reads it, playing absentmindedly with some locks of hair behind his ear. I remember him doing that as a kid. I always scolded him for it. Now I can't remember why it bothered me so much.

As I get closer, I can see the book is a *chumash*, one of the five books of the Pentateuch. The familiar large square print is at the top half of each page, with the vowel dots and cantillation signs. Below is Rashi's commentary, printed in its unique font. When I am within touching distance, I see Nir is reading *chumash Bereshit*, Genesis. Or maybe he is not reading but just staring at it? I can't tell.

What should I do next? I am afraid to scare him off. If I sit down next to him, he might bolt up and start walking again, who knows where to. I would have to continue following him, and at this point I need some rest. Hesitantly, I flip down a seat two spots from him. The hinges are old and rusty, screaming their disagreement. In the empty hollow of the deserted building, the sound is ominous. Nir doesn't seem to notice. I sit down, my body twists toward him, my right elbow resting on the lectern in front of me. The light glows around us, the farther corners of the synagogue in darkness.

I look behind Nir's shoulder, trying not to stir too much. At the top of the page I read:

Vayikchuhu, vayashlichu oto ha'borah, ve'habor reik ein bo ma'yim.

And they took him, and cast him into the pit, and the pit was empty, there was no water in it.

The story of the brothers of Joseph selling him to the Ishmaelites, who then took him to Egypt. I follow Nir's gaze to see what he is reading. The Rashi on the verse. I don't have to read his commentary, I know what it says: *If the pit was empty, don't we know it didn't have water? Why was it necessary to explicitly say there was no water in it? To teach us it had something else in it: snakes and scorpions.*

Snakes and scorpions.

The mysterious light in the dark synagogue seems to penetrate my head, illuminating it from within. At the same time, a movement is in my fist. I open it and recoil violently. A scorpion. I blink. No, just the tail and the fat rounded part with the hard stinger at its end is coiled in my palm, moving slightly. I utter a small, involuntary gasp as I shake my hand to drop it.

The light around me disappears, and with it Nir and his book, the rows of wooden lecterns and seats, the old synagogue. I am back home in my bed, alone. In front of me, on the scrunched-up blanket, lies not a scorpion stinger but the little stone.

∗∗∗

And I remember that *Shabbat* as if it happened yesterday.

Nir was about eight years old. Every *Shabbat* afternoon, thirty minutes before *Mincha*, we went together to a study group for fathers and sons, where we learned the section of the *Torah* read that day in the synagogue. During that *Shabbat*, the weekly portion would be *Vayeshev*, And He Sat. It detailed the stories of Joseph, his father's love and the multicolored coat he made for him, Joseph's prophetic dreams, his brothers' jealousy which eventually led them to sell him to the merchants on their way to Egypt. This eventually brought the entire Israelite clan to Egypt and their enslavement there for hundreds of years. Before selling him off, Judah, one of the brothers, convinced his siblings to throw Joseph into a desert pit instead of killing him, which had been their original plan.

Nir would read the *Torah* verses while I read Rashi's commentaries. Were we sitting in the same spots where I just saw him? I can't tell. Maybe. It was the last time Nir agreed to go. I love all my children the same way, but deep in my heart, I must admit—while I tremendously enjoyed these sessions with Ram when he was younger, I dreaded going with Nir. We never had the same bond, that special connection.

Around us other fathers and sons studied, backs hunched over their books, heads together, almost touching. After some time, old Rabbi Ashlag took a sip of his hot tea and cleared his throat.

"So, who learned the weekly portion?" he asked.

The boys raised their hands, eager to answer and show how smart they were. Some stood on their feet, anxious to be called on.

"Very nice," old Rabbi Ashlag took another sip. "And Rashi, did you read him as well? Do you know what he says?"

The boys nodded, their fathers proud of their compliance.

"Good. So, who wants to tell me something that Rashi said?"

Again, they all raised their hands excitedly. Nir raised his hand without a fuss.

"You, Nir."

Nir stood, head bowed, looking at his hands. He recited the Rashi we had just learned, the one I saw him reading today, and his voice was steady and strong. "Rashi teaches that although the pit was empty from water, it was full with snakes and scorpions." He sat down.

"Very nice. But what does it mean?" Old Rabbi Ashlag raised his bushy eyebrows in question.

Nir rose again. This time, sure of himself, he raised his head toward his classmates. "That Joseph's brothers wanted him to die. They didn't want to murder him, because then their sin would be *Lo Tirtzach*, thou shalt not murder. So instead they put him in the pit with the venomous snakes and scorpions so that he would be killed by their poison."

Old Rabbi Ashlag nodded. He stroked his long beard with one hand, taking off his thick-rimmed glasses with the other. "And what do you think? Did they sin by putting him in the pit?"

"Yes, of course they sinned," Nir replied without hesitation.

The old rabbi leaned forward and rose to his feet, the hand holding the glasses struck the table. "*Shomu Shama'yim!*" he bellowed. "Jacob's sons were *Tzadikim*, righteous men. They didn't sin! Our forefathers, they were the greatest and lived a life of holiness and righteousness!" Rabbi Ashlag wiped his forehead with the back of his hand. "Joseph's brothers were part of God's plan, to fulfill His promise to *Avraham Avinu*, Abraham the patriarch, that his descendants will go to Egypt and be slaves there, and then God would free them and bring them to the promised land..."

His face red, his eyes bulging, old Rabbi Ashlag panted, looking around at the boys. Some of the fathers were nodding their heads, while others were taken aback, surprised by the furious reply to the young boy. They looked at each other, shifting in their seats in discomfort.

Nir looked at me. At first, I thought he would keep standing and try to reply to the old man's wrath. But then he saw me, my expression scolding him silently for his *chutzpah*, his act of standing against a wise old rabbi, not showing the respect I expected of him. He hesitated, one tear shining at the corner of his eye. Then, he slammed the *chumash* closed and ran out of the synagogue through the back door, leading to a narrow alley.

I didn't follow him. I murmured my apology to old Rabbi Ashlag and the other men in the study group, opened the *chumash* to the same place, and buried my head between its pages.

After *Ma'ariv* that night, when I returned home, I made the *Havdallah* like on any other Saturday night. Once I completed the blessings on the wine, essence and light, and the final one dividing the holy *Shabbat* from the rest of the week, Sarah started tidying up the house. She cleared the dining table from the white tablecloth she used for *Shabbat* and holidays, folded it, careful not to drop any of the crumbs on the floor, took it to the wide windows at the service balcony adjacent to the kitchen, and shook it off outside. She then threw it into the hamper with the rest of the dirty *Shabbat* laundry—the boys' white shirts and Millie's dress, the hand towels, and the fabric kerchief I used only during *Shabbat*. Next, she was at the kitchen sink, washing all the dishes that piled up during the day. She liked to plan her week while laboring on the china and silverware, and she found it a good time to go over things with me.

By her clipped movements, the bangs of pans and pots, the rushed way she was doing this work, I sensed she was upset. I didn't say a word; just waited for her to calm down and collect her thoughts. I sat down to read the weekend paper.

"He came home upset from *Shul*," she said, using the Yiddish word her father always used, referring to the synagogue. "Early. I asked him what happened, but he refused to tell me."

"He was quite impertinent today," I said, "to the rabbi."

"What? I don't believe that. Not my Niri!" She turned to look at me, shaking her head. The water ran in the sink while she held a suds-covered dish in her hand. "What was it about?"

I told her what happened.

"And you didn't say anything? Tell this old rabbi there are many ways to learn the *Torah*?" she raised her voice. Now she had completely forgotten about the dishes and the running water behind her. She placed the dish on the counter and picked up a hand towel to dry her hands. "What is this nonsense about everyone in the *Torah* being righteous, no one sinning? Of course they sinned! They all did! Didn't David sin with Bathsheba? Didn't Moshe sin by hitting the rock to get water and God punished him, not letting him enter *Eretz Israel*?"

"It was not the place nor the time for such a discussion," I tried to explain. "It's a simple class for boys, not philosophy arguments of the *yeshiva*!" Why she was always making such a fuss, I couldn't understand. I was there, and Nir practically shamed me. I stood, pushing the chair abruptly, and turned to the sink. Sarah left the water running as if it costs nothing! I turned the water off.

"It is precisely the time!" she said, raising her hands and storming out of the kitchen. "Every lesson is a lesson for life. What do you think he will think now?" She went to the boys' room.

"Nir, Niri, honey," she called, walking into his room as I followed her, reluctantly. He was lying on his stomach, an open book on the floor at the feet of his bed, head poking over the side of the bed to read. "Nir." She sat next to him, pushing him gently to allow for space. "Whatever Rabbi Ashlag said, it seemed to make you upset. He is an old man, and we need to respect him for all the years he studied *Torah*. He is a smart and kind person, and he is very respectable in the community. But he can be wrong too, and that is the lesson the *Torah* is teaching us in many places. That people are people, only flesh and blood, and they can make mistakes. No one is completely righteous without any blemish or sin."

Nir raised his head, leaning on his elbows. He looked at her, his eyes red. He was crying.

"My darling," Sarah cupped his face in her hands, stroking his hair. Nir rested his head on her lap and closed his eyes, the corners of his mouth turning into a smile.

When she rose to leave the room, he looked at me. His smile disappeared.

Today, on the windy beach, I saw this look again.

CHAPTER 5

Tuesday, Third Day of the Shiva

RAM

The next day, the *shiva* routine continued.

His father woke up close to noon. He looked as if old age had taken over him during the night, but he insisted on joining Ram and Millie at the *shiva* seat. He was quieter than usual, nodding his head rather than joining in conversations, sighing heavily, supporting his head with his hand as if it would otherwise fall off.

All day long people came in and out. Chaim's old friends with their spouses, his coworkers at the accounting firm, Sarah's friends, the group she met with until she became ill. Every Wednesday night they had baked together and exchanged recipes. Millie's girlfriends came in large groups, along with teachers and rabbis from her *ulpana* high school. Ram's colleagues came from the army and some childhood friends. Nir's high school classmates came too; Ram recognized some of them.

There was just one person Ram was looking forward to seeing: Tammy. For the funeral, he had begged her not to come. He knew how much he needed her there and how wonderful she would have been. He could have leaned on her for support, she would have understood his pain. But he knew it would be the wrong time to introduce her to his family, or what was left of it.

Tammy, the *kibbutznik* tomboy, grew-up in the south in a kibbutz affiliated with the *Hashomer Hatzair* movement, as far left and as opposite as possible from the family and environment he had grown up in. She spent her childhood in the *Beit Yeladim*, the children's house, seeing her parents for an hour each weekday and on weekends. She showered with girls and boys her age, not worrying about modesty. Ram knew she had had a couple of boyfriends before him, and that was normal in the world she came from. Food in the kibbutz dining room was far from being kosher by any definition. He still cringed, a childhood habit from growing up in a kosher-observant home, every time she mentioned the kibbutz's culinary combinations—grilled chicken and buttered potatoes, sandwiches with slices of salami and yellow cheese, and ham, a.k.a. white-meat, on special occasions.

Sometimes Ram felt like he came from a different planet. Orthodox family, keeping kosher, going to an all-boys religious school—that's what Ram had known his whole life. Even in Bnei Akiva, where girls participated in some of the youth group's activities alongside the boys, they were careful to keep their distance. No touching. No joking around. Jewish lessons were part of every activity. On the few cinema nights, the movies were censored; the projector operator abruptly skipped over any scene with a hint of sexual content.

During his senior year of *yeshiva* high school, he nursed some nagging questions about religious practices and philosophical wonderings about life. But he kept them to himself, afraid to explore them, terrified of what would happen if he did. Instead, he wanted to grow stronger in his beliefs and devotion to the God he knew and grew up with. So, when he graduated, he joined a *Hesder Yeshiva*. This *yeshiva* took part in the arrangement between the religious political parties and the army. The students divided their time between active service in the infantry or armored corps and *yeshiva* periods, learning *Talmud* and other religious studies. During the ten long months he spent there, he saw how many of his classmates and close friends became entranced with their studies, putting religion and the *Halacha*, the religious law, before anything else—before their families, their ambitions, their self-worth. He didn't want to become like them, to blindly follow everything their rabbis told them. He wanted to *think* on his own.

But the turning point was when his mother passed away. Everyone at the *yeshiva* seemed to be there for him during the *shiva*—his classmates, the rabbis, students of the other classes. The message from all was the same: God is great, and God works in mysterious ways, and God has his plan and His plan was to take Ram's mother. He had tried so hard to accept it. To thank his God for his unexplained, merciless ways. But he missed his mother too much.

Yes, they knew it was her final days. The treatments had failed, and she could not win against the aggressive cancer. But… There was always a "but"! But he had prayed to God to heal her. They had *all* prayed; his father, Nir, and Millie. Their family and all their friends. His father's synagogue and his *yeshiva* had arranged a marathon prayer vigil on the eve of her last day, where special prayers were chanted and Psalm chapters recited. They even went to a famous rabbi, a Kabbalist who blessed people from near and far, and who promised them she would heal and be present in her grandchildren's weddings. Nothing helped.

Ram returned to the *yeshiva* after the long *shiva* week, defeated and stricken. The studies he had left the week before meant nothing now. He spent most of the time on his own, in one corner of the study hall, learning the *Mishnah* chapters for his mother's soul. The learning worked the opposite way of the old sages' intention; instead of calming his mind and bringing him back to the *Torah*'s golden path, he grew angrier at the God who had not heard his prayers.

So, when the *yeshiva* period ended, and it was time to start his first army service term with his classmates, he decided to quit the *Hesder* program and join the general army forces. He mingled with people from other backgrounds—secular Jews, Druze, females, young men and women from across the country—and his old doubts resurfaced. Doubts about his place in the world, about the stressful relationship between religion and science, about answers that his rabbis would offhandedly give for contradictions in the Bible: "Nothing is early or late in the *Torah*," was their reply where chronological order did not make sense in the *Torah* stories. "It's the law as given to Moses on Mount Sinai," they would say if there was no apparent reason for a specific law. And the kicker, the one fallback response for anything they could not explain—"We cannot understand God. Our human capacity is too limited."

But how could he let it all go? It was all he knew: his father's ethics and his mother's teachings. The deterioration in his belief system was slow and painful, yet inevitable.

He found comfort in new friendships formed during their collective experience keeping their homeland safe. As rough and blunt as some of his new friends were, they respected him, treated him as an equal, never let him feel they were better than him. The glass bubble he had grown up in his entire life shuttered, gradually, piece by piece. Unlike the patronizing, we-are-better-than-them attitude of many of his rabbis and *yeshiva* friends, his father and community, Ram saw the beauty in his new friends' diversity and acceptance. Not that they were all perfect. But who was?

And then there was Tammy. Darling Tammy.

***

TAMMY

Tammy came to the funeral despite Ram's request. How could she stay away? It was one thing to try to understand Ram's upbringing and be patient with the small stuff, like when he flinched every time he saw her eating seafood or when his hand involuntarily rose to check if his *kippah* was still on his bare head. It made him more special in her eyes: different from anyone she loved before. But to stay away from his brother's funeral? How could she live with herself knowing she wasn't there for him?

She wore the most modest clothes she owned, a black long-sleeved blouse she usually wore unbuttoned, revealing a white tight tank top and a pair of dark jeans. This time she buttoned the shirt, and to be on the safe side, she threw a light sweater on top of it. Although it was late October, the day was reaching a summer-like sizzling point.

When she arrived at the cemetery entrance, she realized how out of place she felt. The women stood separately from the men, most of them huddled in small groups, talking in low voices. Almost all the women wore some head covering— hats or scarves tied around their hair. She couldn't spot any woman wearing pants; they all wore long skirts or dresses. Several of them turned their heads to look at her, then turned back to speak with their friends. *Why didn't I come in uniform?* She was afraid the army greens would offend some of the more religious in the crowd, but now she regretted that decision. At least it would have been acceptable that female soldiers do wear pants.

Tammy walked around to the edge of the crowd. She avoided the looks and focused on what she was there for—supporting Ram. She craned her neck and searched for him, but she couldn't see him through the dense gathering. The group of men in the front started walking, the women following behind, shuffling their feet on the gravel. Tammy walked with them. She thought she saw Ram's back at the front of the crowd, but she wasn't sure. All the men wore *kippahs* or hats, and it was hard to tell them apart. She gave up trying when they reached the fresh grave plot, and the procession came to a halt. Sweat ran down her nape, her undershirt stuck to her body. She didn't dare to remove her top blouse and attract unnecessary attention. It was so hot.

The rectangular burial place where they lowered Nir into was in the middle of a long row of graves, all taken and covered with white marble slabs and headstones. Soldiers and young men stood amongst the graves, in the narrowest gaps between them. The gravel lane they walked on was filled with people, standing in a large semicircle, split almost evenly between men and women.

Tammy contemplated waiting until the burial was over for people to walk back the way they came. Ram might be standing on his own next to the fresh grave. But this was a religious funeral, she reminded herself, light years from the romantic vision of funerals in movies. So she dismissed the idea, hoping Ram felt she was with him. She turned around with the crowd and found her way out.

On the morning of the third day of the *shiva*, Tammy reached the building on the outskirts of Bnei Brak. She walked from the station where the bus had dropped her, along with a loud group of school kids who ran around her, shouting to each other in Yiddish. Their old-fashioned school bags bounced on their backs, while their tangled sidelocks, some so long they reached their shoulders, ruffled on both sides of their heads. An old woman in head-to-toes black attire pushed a black-canvas shopping cart in front of her. With one hand, she scolded two of the boys who ran right by her while her face was still smiling. Tammy caught herself staring. She quickly averted her eyes, her hand checking for the hundredth time that she had buttoned her blouse all the way up. She caught a glimpse of her reflection in one of the parked cars.

She didn't know what to expect. At the kibbutz, people choose how they want to mourn the death of their loved ones. Some had communal singing events in their memory, playing and singing the Israeli songs they loved. Others wanted a quiet service and asked that no one outside of the immediate family show up. Most people didn't sit *shiva* or take more than a day or two off from work. The cows had to be milked, and the fields wouldn't wait 'til next year for plowing or picking.

The four storied building was close to the bus station. Tammy couldn't tell how old it was. It looked like a thousand other apartment buildings, gray and dirty with years of city pollution. It stood on rows of skinny concrete columns, hovering over some battered cars parking between them. A neglected entry had only a doorpost, the door was missing. A black-on-white obituary sign was taped on the wall. *This is where Ram had grown up*, Tammy thought, a knot building in her throat. She stepped inside and into a dark lobby. To her right was a row of old and crooked mail slots, and to her left, a chipped mirror covering half of the wall. Another obituary sign hung at the corner of the mirror.

The staircase was gloomy. Barely any light reached it from the entrance door. *How can people live like this?* She could never understand. To her, living in one of these apartments was equal to boxing oneself in a metal and concrete block with hundreds of people. She craved the vast fields surrounding her childhood's kibbutz, the fresh smell of grass and manure, the deep blue skies that stretched across the horizon, the low calls of the grazing cows.

She stumbled in the dark, looking for the light switch. When she found it and pushed it on, a faint light bulb illuminated the way up. Ram's family lived on the top floor. She looked for an elevator and pushed the only other door in the lobby, but it led to a narrow set of stairs going down. A sharp stench of fermented garbage floated up her way. So she took the stairs, skipping them by twos.

She was short of breath by the time she reached the fourth-floor landing, but it was worth it. She could feel her nerves were now under control. The door to Ram's home was slightly ajar, the security bracket hinged outward, blocking the door from shutting firmly. The same sign, bold letters on simple paper, was taped to the door:

**BLESSED IS HE WHO JUDGES TRUE
WITH HEAVY HEARTS WE ANNOUNCE
THE DEATH OF
NIR LEVI Z"L
SON OF CHAIM AND SARAH Z"L LEVI
BROTHER TO RAM AND MILLIE
THE GRIEVING FAMILY**

What a shame, she thought. Ram didn't speak about Nir often, but when he did he spoke of how much he missed him, worried if he would find his way, and the rift between Nir and their father. He cared for his brother like a parent. *It wasn't right*, she always wanted to shout. *You have your father, and he is not doing his job, the bastard! You shouldn't have to be Nir's brother* and *father.* But she said nothing. She knew where such an outburst would take them. Ram would try to justify his father's position yet appease her. And she definitely didn't want him to do that. So she took some distance, holding back on interfering in Ram's family affairs. She didn't expect them to unfold the way they did. Who would expect an end like this? Thinking of the struggle Nir must have had in the rough sea, chills traveled up her spine.

Tammy entered the apartment. She hoped to see someone familiar from the army to put her at ease. Tzipi and Shlomi, two of their friends from the base, had offered to travel with her. They planned to arrive in the evening after finishing the workday, but she was too anxious to wait, and now she regretted her decision. She searched for Ram, and when she didn't see him in the living room or at the dining table, she continued to the kitchen.

Crossing the threshold felt like entering a cave-like cabin that stood in the middle of a sun-drowned field. The living room behind her was washed with endless sunlight from the open glass windows, the light reflecting from the bare white walls and stone floor. In contrast, the kitchen was choked floor to ceiling with dark wood cabinets, black granite slab countertops, and a dark ceramic floor. The small window above the stove did a poor job of allowing much light in, and the only artificial light came from a single bulb above the table nook. Tupperware containers of every size and shape were piled everywhere—on the table, the counters, the open shelves.

"Can I help you?" a middle-aged woman turned from the stove to ask her. She held a knife in one hand and a piece of sponge cake in the other. A teenage girl sat at the table, her face buried in an open *siddur*. Tammy's eyes adjusted to the dimness. The girl's shirt was slightly torn to the right of her neck, the cloth tacked together with a safety pin. In front of her, between the stacks of plastic boxes, the girl had a plate with food. It was untouched.

"Yes," Tammy said.

The woman didn't wait for her to ask for Ram. "Are you one of Millie's friends?"

"Millie?"

The girl lifted her eyes from the pages. They were glazed and red, void of recognition. She turned back to her book.

"No, no," Tammy finally said. "I am here for Ram."

"Ram is with his father in the bedroom." The older woman put the knife and cake down on the counter and wiped her hands with her apron. "Dr. Frisch is here to check up on him. He will be done soon."

"Is he all right?" Tammy stepped closer.

"Yes, yes, God willing. He will be fine. Just stress and too many people around..." Her voice trailed. "I am Chava, Ram's aunt." She stretched her hand out in greeting.

Tammy wasn't sure what to do, both her hands tucked deeply in her jeans' back pockets.

"It's okay. You can shake hands with me," Chava said, a wide smile in her eyes.

Tammy blushed. She was confused about the rules. Is it only religious men who don't shake women's hands, or also religious women? Maybe they don't shake any secular people hands? She wondered when she would know the right thing to do. She took Chava's hand and shook it, immediately feeling relieved.

"I'm Tammy," she introduced herself. "Here, this is for you." She handed Chava a plastic bag from the *Sufersal*. She had bought some *bourekas* on her way to the house, making sure they were kosher. She stayed with the potato variety, just to be on the safe side—it had neither meat nor dairy ingredients. No reason to take a risk in something she knew so little about.

"Thank you. You really shouldn't have, but I appreciate it." Chava looked in the bag. "We can put these to some good use! *Baruch HaShem*, they didn't lose their appetite, and with all the people coming over..."

"Can I help you with anything while I am waiting for Ram?" Tammy asked. She fidgeted in place, unsure whether she should sit or stand, go back to the living room or hide in the kitchen. She wanted to see Ram and hold him tightly, but that would have to wait.

"Sure. Why don't you put these in the fridge and help me with the cakes? You would think it was someone's birthday if you didn't know otherwise! I don't know what people think. They need to eat food, not just cakes!"

Tammy liked Chava. Her kind face and warm welcome, even in these circumstances, reminded her of Shosh, her nursery teacher. She had been her surrogate mother, and her passing away had opened a wound in her heart.

Shosh was the face she saw when she woke up, shining at her first thing in the morning. She would come to her bed, open her arms, her full bosom ready to accept Tammy's warm body, her smell like fresh baked bread and cinnamon. Shosh was the last face she gave a good night kiss to every night at the children's house. Her tired face bursting in a huge smile, wishing Tammy, "Good night my *bubbale*. Sweet dreams, my little one."

On the days that her parents didn't show up to pick her up and take her to their room—she forgot now how often that happened—Shosh would keep her by her side. She tagged along, mimicking everything Shosh did. She would shuffle the toy-chairs in the dolls' corner when Shosh arranged the kids' chairs. While Shosh collected the dirty plastic dishes and washed them in the large stainless-steel basin, Tammy air-washed the toy dishes under the faucet that the kibbutz's plumber installed for them to play with. She asked Shosh to tie a clean cloth diaper around her waist. This way, she was ready to work, just like Shosh with her white apron.

Shosh gave undivided attention to each and every kid at the children's house, and they all felt special; they all loved Shosh. For Tammy, it was more than loving a dear caregiver—she loved Shosh like her own imma. Sometimes, more than her own imma.

When Shosh fell sick, she suffered one mysterious virus after another. Tammy was at her side every night or morning, first in the kibbutz's clinic, and later at the hospital, when more excessive treatment was called for. Eventually her aged body gave up. She passed away with a smile on her old face, surrounded by many of the children who were like her own.

Tammy missed Shosh, more than she had ever missed anyone.

***

She heard men's voices from the living room. Tammy hoped it might mean Ram was out of his father's room and she could finally see him.

"Reb Chaim," one voice said. "*Baruch rofeh cholim.*" Blessed is He who heals the sick. "*Baruch HaShem*, we see you on your feet again. We were worried!"

"Let him be," said another.

"Abba, I'll be right back. I'll bring you some juice and chocolate *rugelach* from the kitchen." Tammy's heart missed a beat when she heard Ram's voice. She waited patiently in the kitchen, but instead another person came in. He opened the fridge, took out an orange juice carton, and poured some into a clear glass, while Chava took several crescent-shaped pastries from a plastic container, put them on a plate, and handed it over to the man. He thanked her, looked quizzically at Tammy, and returned to the living room.

She followed him, unsure yet why it hadn't been Ram that came in to get the refreshments for his dad. *Kibud horim*, the *mitzvah* of respecting thy father and mother, was so important to Ram. This is why, he had explained many times, he didn't tell his father he left the *Hesder Yeshiva* for religious reasons. Instead, his official reason was that he wanted to finish his army service and start his university studies. He preferred to tell white lies rather than hurt his father's feelings. He hid the fact that he didn't believe in God anymore, that he removed his *kippah* and stopped keeping kosher, that he didn't observe the *Shabbat*, and that he had a girlfriend—a *chiloni*, secular, girlfriend.

At first, he didn't notice her. His attention was on the older man she assumed was his father. The way they sat on the old sofa, with their bodies low and their knees projecting high, reminded Tammy of people from the city sitting at the back of a farmer's pickup truck, misfit in their unnatural environment. The man had a similar build to Ram's, although stockier. Like Ram, he was unshaven, his thinning hair mostly gray and peppered with black, looking as if he had just gotten out of bed. Deep lines crossed his face, from his nose to the base of his jaw, across his brow and the corners of his eyes. His chin sagged. Ram was looking at him with worried eyes while the man she followed from the kitchen gave him the glass and placed the plate on an empty chair.

Ram looked up and saw her. He smiled briefly at her. In that split second she saw his body relax then tense up again. He glanced at his father, checking his reaction. He then stood, and with two strides he reached her.

"Tammy, I'm so glad you came!" He didn't reach out to kiss or hug her, so she froze in place, forcing her body to stay still. How she would have loved to wrap her hands around him at that moment, to smell his familiar scent and feel his warmth close to her. She understood from his tone of voice, from the urgent flicker in his eyes, that it was neither the time nor the place. He was right, but it still caught her by surprise.

"Of course! I mi—" she paused to correct herself. "We all miss you at the base." Then, as an afterthought, she felt obliged to add, "I'm sorry I couldn't come to the funeral. I had something urgent to deal with. You know how Klaussner is." She raised her voice, glancing at the people in the room, gauging for any raised brows, any unaccepting glances. When she saw none, she felt lighter. The words felt flat in her mouth, but she knew how worried Ram would be about being appropriate, so she did it for his sake. No need to add additional stress to the already stressful situation.

"Come. We can go to my room," Ram surprised her, and to his father and the men around him he added, "If any of my friends arrive, just send them to my room, okay?" Not waiting for a reply he turned on his heel, Tammy following behind.

They walked to his room, which was just a closed off balcony behind another bedroom. He left the door to the room open. The green plastic shutters were mostly closed, hidden behind brown glass panels that kept the room cool from the blazing sun. He slid one of the panels to the right and raised the levers on some shutters, twisting them open and letting light in. A single sofa bed was tucked neatly against the back corner. A beige Formica desk stood next to it, and a couple of matching shelves hung on the wall above the bed. An old wooden cupboard was the only other furniture in the room. It was tall and narrow, and its side was haphazardly decorated with a collection of yellowing paper clippings. The desk and shelves were covered with textbooks, Jewish-studies books, some old Israeli travel books, and comics.

Right next to the bed, on the only empty spot on the desk, stood a single plain picture frame. In it, a young Ram, maybe ten or eleven, smiled at her. He stood on a rock, wearing short pants and a blue shirt, his skinny legs firmly planted in place. Next to him, a beautiful woman looked at the camera. Her arm hugged Ram's slender shoulder. They had the same smile.

For a brief moment Tammy felt like a teenager again, invading his old room. A thin layer of dust covered the desk, the books, and the picture frame.

Ram dropped heavily on the sofa bed. "Come, sit here," he patted the firm mattress next to him.

"Are you sure?" she hesitated.

He nodded slowly, his eyes blinking with every movement of his head. "I'm tired of this. All of this." He spread his hands to his sides, a desperate gesture trying to demonstrate what all of *this* meant.

She sat beside him and allowed him to make whatever move he was comfortable with. He hugged her. His hold was strong, desperate. Even though she knew he hadn't showered or shaved since the funeral, she loved the way he smelled, like sweet cacao and worn flannel.

Ram leaned into her and softened in her arms. Now she was the strong one, holding him, comforting him. Sitting quietly for a few minutes, they didn't have to say a word.

"Shhh, it will be fine. Everything will be fine..." she whispered. His body heaved in her arms. He was crying. She put her hand on his head, caressing his short hair. Her fingers tangled with the *kippah* on his head. She stroked him around it, her fingers adjusting, giving it space.

They stayed like that for several minutes; she didn't know exactly how long. He then wiped his face with the back of his hand, trying to pull himself together.

"This is so hard," he said in a hoarse voice. "The way he died, Imma not being here with us... My abba is breaking up... He fainted yesterday and then he was talking about Nir, but none of it made any sense."

Tammy nodded. She'd had her share of loss, growing up with an absent mother and, more recently, losing Shosh. She knew the endless thoughts of loss tangled in the head and the bottomless void opened in the heart.

"I don't know when things will get better," she said, "but I know they will. It's such a cliché, and I hated hearing it myself, but here I am repeating it. So I guess it's true."

Ram looked at her, his eyes red and wet.

"I don't know how my dad will live with the knowledge that he didn't talk with Nir—" Ram groaned. He shook his head, holding Tammy's hands in his. "They didn't speak for almost two years! Two years!"

Tammy nodded. She knew there was a serious rift between Ram's father and brother but didn't know the details. He didn't like talking about it. When she tried to offer help, he dismissed her, saying that nothing can help these two mules. They were stubborn, especially his dad, and they could never agree on anything.

"Yes! Two fucking years! It's a lifetime for some of us! What did he think?" Ram's voice rose, and his face reddened. "That Nir would live forever and eventually God would put some sense into him?"

Tammy could not remember a time he ever cursed like that. She did not interrupt his venting.

"At first, we tried to talk to my dad, to make him change his mind. Who didn't we speak with to intervene? Chava and her husband... Some of his friends... Rabbi Zechariah... But Abba didn't want to hear. 'Not over my dead body,'" Ram mimicked his dad, his voice lower and grumpy, the corners of his mouth dropping slightly. "'I said he is dead to me, and I meant it. You should not mention his name in this house again. You hear me?'" Ram covered his face with his hands, his back hunched over. He shook his head violently. "He once got so upset, he couldn't stand and had to lie down, took a pill to relax his nerves, and asked everyone to leave him alone. It was the same every time someone approached him with the subject."

And now, Tammy thought what Ram would not say aloud, *it was too late.*

"In the first few months," Ram continued, "he told Millie and me that we couldn't talk with Nir. He wanted us to cut him off completely. He thought it would help in changing Nir, but he didn't see the flaw in his plan; the only one he punished was himself."

"Did you do it?" Tammy asked.

"*Ma pitom!* Are you crazy? No way. I would never do something like that. Loving someone is accepting them, not forcing them to be just like you!" He jumped to his feet, restless. Deep inside Tammy was happy. This was the man she was falling in love with, and he gave her more reasons to love him every day. She didn't understand him yet, not completely, but who understood anybody fully?

"I didn't think you would," she said, "but with *kibud horim* and all that, I thought you or Millie might have... I'm sorry."

"No, we didn't. We didn't tell him what we were doing every second, and we would talk with Nir all the time, go out with him, try to cheer him up. We wanted to help but we didn't know how."

Ram turned around, his back to her. He stopped by the window. With one hand, he widened the gap between two shutters, looking outside. The sun was high in the sky, and it washed the buildings across the street in bright colors. His arm still raised and holding the shutter, Ram lowered his head, his forehead resting on his forearm. Silently, Tammy stood behind him and closed her arms around his chest. She let him be. He could tell her more some other time when he felt like talking. For now, they stood silently together in her embrace.

***

RAM

"Ram, some people want to see you." Millie stood at the door. They hadn't heard her approaching. The door was open, and she just stood there, waiting.

"I will be there in a minute," Ram said, rising from the sofa bed, a bit too fast. He almost lost his balance, so he reached for the desk and leaned on it to prevent his fall. He felt heat rushing up his ears, fueled by a fundamental gut instinct that he and Tammy had done something wrong. Then Ram reminded himself that he had done *nothing* wrong. That he shouldn't care so much what other people think. But Millie wasn't just other people. And he wanted her to like Tammy. At least she had not seen them hugging by the shutters. By now they were just sitting on the sofa, talking like two friends.

Tammy stood as well in one slow motion, steady on her feet. She stretched her hand out to Millie.

"Hi," she said, "I'm Tammy. I'm a friend of Ram. From the army…" she hesitated. "You're Millie, right?"

"Yes." Millie ignored her hand and backed the way she came, almost forgetting to turn around on her heels.

"I'm sorry," Ram said. "This is not how I wanted you to meet my family."

"You have nothing to be sorry about." When he didn't reply, she added, "Are you worried about what she thinks about us?"

How well she knows me, he thought. "It's stupid."

"No, it's not." Tammy lifted her hand to hold his chin. She held his gaze with hers, and very slowly she said, "I love you, Lieutenant Ram Levi. No matter who your family is and what they think of me. *You* are the man I'm falling in love with. Remember that."

Even though the door was open and anyone could come in, Ram held Tammy in a long embrace, drawing from her strength. "I love you too," he whispered in her ear. "Thank you for being here."

When he finally let go, Ram excused himself and went to wash his face in the bathroom. He hated the itching bristles, the torn shirt he had to wear every day of the *shiva*, the constant flow of visitors, and that he couldn't do anything about it. Looking at the mirror, he saw worn brown eyes looking back, puffy, bloodshot.

Tammy waited outside the bathroom, and when he finished, she followed him to the living room. Although it was an early afternoon hour, the apartment already felt cramped and stifled with visitors. *The place will be packed toward* Mincha *time*, Ram thought. *I hope Abba will be okay with that.*

When he saw his father, Ram relaxed slightly. Chaim was at the center of attention, exactly where he liked being. A small crowd of early retired friends and their wives—mostly homemakers who had left their jobs as secretaries or clerks after their firstborn arrived—flocked Chaim around the brown sofa, laughing at a remark someone made. Ram knew most of them. He had grown up with their children and attended the same schools. Their families were members of the same synagogue. And since the children's generation had started getting married and having their babies, the parents' main activity was meeting at each other's celebrations.

A man from the group noticed him. "Ram, so good to see you!" he called out. "Although in such tragic circumstances! Come, sit with us." They shuffled their chairs around, letting him through into their circle.

Ram turned to look at Tammy. "I have to sit with my dad."

"Go ahead; it's okay." She nodded and gestured for him that she understood. She smiled when he smiled at her.

Ram left Tammy behind and sat next to his father on the mourners' low sofa. Some of his father's friends noticed Tammy and exchanged knowing or puzzled glances.

"Can I get you something, dear?" It was Mrs. Schwartz. She gently straightened her *sheitel*, a fashionable shoulder-length blond wig. She always had a kind smile for Ram and his siblings.

"Thank you. Something hot to drink would be nice," Ram said.

"Right away! I will make you a nana-mint tea. It will make you feel so much better! And I brought some cake. Do you remember my layered coffee cake?" She flashed her famous smile and hurried to the kitchen.

"So, what were we talking about? Oh, yes. Listen to this, Ram," Chaim said, still smiling, gripping Ram's arm. "Simcha here was telling us about his son's officer graduation ceremony last week in Mitzpe Ramon. They almost lost their way like we did on our way to Eilat. Do you remember that?" He chuckled.

Ram remembered. How could he forget after hearing it so many times? He also knew his father would tell the story nevertheless. He probably had told it just before Ram came from the room. And who knows, he might have repeated it several times this week since the *shiva* started. But if this could distract his father's mind for the moment, Ram didn't mind being subjected to hearing it again.

As if reading his thoughts, Chaim began the story. "So, we were driving along road number forty from Be'er Sheva, nothing around us, just sand and rocks and some more sand. The sun was high in the sky, and it was hot! But dry, very dry heat!"

"Yes, of course it's dry heat," someone said. "So much better than the hundred percent humidity we have here, I am telling you!"

Chaim ignored the comment. "There were some Bedouin shacks in the distance, along the ridge of a ravine, and we could see kids playing with some rocks, throwing them at a derelict junk car. They were supposed to watch their goats and sheep, but you know how these Bedouins are. The animals were grazing right next to the road. For the life of me,

I don't know what they were eating exactly. I didn't see any grass there. Maybe some old truck tires?

"Just before we reached that stretch, one of the ugly beasts charged into the asphalt. I barely slammed the brakes, almost hitting it. The car swiveled around, and we were sure we would find ourselves upside down! Sarah screamed. She reached her hands back to you guys to make sure you were okay, blaming *me* for not watching the road."

The women in the living room nodded their heads, their husbands listening intently.

"Then two Bedouin kids ran toward the car, carrying big stones in their hands. I was sure they would throw them at us! You know, the Bedouins are just like all the Arabs: they hate us, and we can't trust them!" Now it was the turn of the men to nod their heads. Ram felt dizzy. It was hard enough to hear his father's stories for the millionth time. He despised the prejudice and generalization of people his father knew nothing about. Ram knew what was coming next.

"The smaller of the two was shouting in Arabic, while the older one, with a mean look on his face, ran and jumped so quickly that he scared away the rest of the herd." Chaim now faced his friends, his hands animated as he told the story. "Before they reached our car, I told Sarah and the kids to duck down and cover their heads. I left the car with our backpack and held it in front of my face for protection. Sarah shouted at me to stay in the car. I still went out! I would protect my family with my life if I had to!"

Chaim's friends were mesmerized, listening to every word that came out of his mouth. Ram suspected most of them had heard this story before.

"I decided to get ready as well, and picked up some stones from the side of the road. If they came and blitzed us with rocks, I would do the same to them! I stacked some into my pockets and a few into the backpack, ignoring the dust and sand. Thorns scraped my hands, and I abandoned all caution and probably disturbed snakes or scorpions from under those rocks—"

Chaim stopped talking. He gazed above his friends' heads, looking at some invisible spot in the air. He held his head with both hands, his entire face shrank in concentration.

Someone from the group said, "Chaim, are you okay?"

"Abba?" Ram reached now to hold his father's arm. A small wave passed through the room while everyone shifted in their seats, bodies tensing.

Before the room erupted in concern, Chaim straightened up, his eyes cleared. His gaze dropped quickly toward the right-hand side pocket of his slacks, which he caressed with several fingers like someone checking that he hadn't lost his keys. Seemingly relieved, he wiped his brow with the back of his hand. "Yes, yes, I'm fine," he said, "If someone could get me some black coffee, it would be great."

Mrs. Schwartz rose again and rushed to the kitchen. Ram didn't notice her returning before with his tea, but now he saw the glass cup on the little coffee table beside the sofa, still steaming.

"Let me tell you what happened next. You hear me?" Chaim's voice was weak, but he clearly was eager to grab their attention again. "I was waiting for them on the road. No other cars were driving by. The sun was blazing and large in the sky. These two bandits ran toward us, shouting like lunatics. Sarah and the kids were crouching in the car, frightened to death, and the only weapon I had were a bunch of stones I just collected from the side of the road!"

"Why didn't you just get out of there?" someone asked from the front row.

"And show them we fear them? No way! I was not afraid, and I was not ready to show them, or my kids, that I am afraid!"

Ram was surprised. It had been a long time since, and it never occurred to him that his father could just have stayed in the car and continued driving. He always thought there was something wrong with the vehicle, and that's what forced Chaim to face those kids.

"So I am standing there, and I am thinking, *Haba le'orgecha—Hashkem le'orgo;* kill or be killed, right?"

Chaim's circle of friends was silent, mesmerized by his story. Mrs. Schwartz handed him the coffee he asked for. He sipped it loudly, another habit Ram couldn't stand but one he'd learned to ignore.

"I told myself, *It's either me or them, my family or these savages!* You hear me? I could see that the smaller of the two—I think they were brothers if one could judge by their bare feet, dirty faces, and long unkempt hair—raised his hand while he was still shouting in Arabic. I raised my hand too and shouted back for them to stop where they were, that I have stones too and was not afraid to use them, raising a hand with a large rock to show them I meant business. Their cries, as well as mine, were carried across the wadi, and I noticed some commotion from their dwellings' direction. A couple of older people ran out of the metal hut, waving their hands. One of them had a walking stick, and she raised it above her head, shaking it crazily from side to side.

"When the two brothers were a stone shot away from the road, I could hear them shout, '*Ma'ez, ma'ez, yejr'e, weqbed 'ela alema'ez,*' or something like that. I don't speak Arabic, but even I could tell what *ma'ez* might mean!" and he burst out laughing, his entire gang of friends joining him. He almost spilled the coffee on his lap, catching it at the last minute.

Ram remembered. It's almost like in Hebrew. *Ma'ez. Ez. Goat.*

"So they ran after a goat? Or after you?" Mrs. Schwartz asked.

"Yes! They were sure I ran over it, but it was grazing just behind the Subaru! When they reached us, the older boy ran around the car in a large circle and the young one dropped to his knees, looking under the wheels for its body. It happened so fast that at first I didn't understand what was going on, thinking they had a bomb and they planned to put it under the car, right in front of my eyes! But you know what? Close up they did look harmless, and when they saw that damn goat, the older boy grabbed it with his bare hands, and they both ran away, back where they came from, shouting, '*Ma'ez, ma'ez, ma'ez.*'"

Rolling laughs filled the living room. A woman peeked out from the kitchen door. She frowned and shook her head, then quickly disappeared.

Chaim turned to Ram. "Do you remember what you and Nir always said after that, every time you saw Bedouins?"

Ram couldn't help but reply, mimicking a younger version of himself, bleating like a goat, "Ma'ez, ma'ez, *ma'eeeez.*"

The laughs erupted again. *It might not be such a bad thing to laugh a bit*, Ram thought, to forget for a few minutes their agony. His father had some color in his face, the wrinkles on his forehead were a tad relaxed.

When the laughs and giggles settled down, Chaim excused himself and left the room. The brown sofa felt bigger now, the air around it momentarily expanding and contracting, filling the void he left behind. The circle of friends broke down into smaller groups. Baruch Langer, an old friend of Chaim, sat beside Ram. He shifted in his chair toward Ram, his hand straightening strands of unruly long white hairs back to their place in his combover. Ram noticed a stain on his buttoned shirt. His breath smelled of onion.

"How are you, Ram? Holding up?" Baruch asked.

"Yes, as much as I can," Ram said.

"And what can you tell us about the situation up north? Any news from the border?"

"Nothing you don't hear on the news," was Ram's careful reply. Many people tried to fish for sensitive information about the situation at the northern border with Lebanon, and he knew how to fend them off.

"Of course, of course," Baruch said. "What is this nonsense your dad is talking about, seeing Nir?"

Ram's face darkened. "What do you mean? Before Nir drowned?"

Baruch looked at Ram. "No, not before he drowned. He is talking about seeing him today."

CHAPTER 6

CHAIM

I am back in my bedroom and it feels safe here. I won't be too long away from my duty at the *shiva*. Can't have people wondering where I've disappeared! But I need a few minutes on my own.

The little stone sits in my pocket. I've put it there myself, wrapped in thin tissue paper, and I can feel it through the fabric of my pants.

I don't remember how I got it, but I think I know now who gave it to me. That man yesterday, right after *Ma'ariv*. He came over and shook my hand, and then slipped the little thing into my palm. I can't explain it any other way. That's when I first saw Nir, so it must be.

How that man got the stone in the first place is still a mystery to me! I am sure I put it on my son's grave. Am I going crazy? No, no! I refuse to accept this judgment. I remember it clearly: the brown dirt, the pine scent. The stone looked so small and lonely on that large mound. So how did that man find it?

Never mind. There is the stone, and this morning, again, I saw Nir, and it was with the little stone in my hand, the little stone that takes me to him.

I sit on the edge of my bed, tears roll down my face. Just a day ago I thought my heart would never heal, that I would never feel normal again. But now I have some hope. I can see him again; it must mean something! And if he is still there, maybe I can save him. Maybe.

I *need* to see him again.

I quickly take the little bundle out of my pocket and unfold the crumpled paper to reveal the stone. In the limited light, it's almost indistinguishable from its surroundings. I pick it up gently between my forefinger and thumb. For a moment I look at it, trying to understand its power. Then, I gingerly close my right palm around it, wrapping it with the left. When it is secured within my palms, I close my eyes.

***

Nir slams the *chumash* closed, startling me, déjà vu tingles through my entire body. He is right there next to me, at the Old Ashlag.

He doesn't move and just sits there, staring at the closed book, six letters printed in dark blue on its light green cover: "*Bet, Resh, Aleph, Shin, Yud, Taf. Bereshit.*" In the beginning. Genesis. His left palm is cupped over something on the table. He slowly raises it, the fingertips still touching the table, protecting whatever he is holding in there. Something crawls from between his fingers—a crab's claw. He reaches with his other hand, palm face up, making a scoop with it. The little creature climbs on it and rests there, fitting just right. Nir bolts upright and rushes to the other side of the bench, looking for the aisle that leads to the back door. While I stumble after him, I notice the cover of the *chumash* has now only five letters, the *Aleph* missing. Now it reads, "Bar Shit."

I do not stop to think about what it means. All I want to do, all I *need* to do, is stay with Nir, not lose him again, make him talk to me, make him forgive me. Save him. I rush out through the back door. Outside, I expect to see the dark marshes, the crooked moon with its strange smile, maybe even the critters. I expect to hear the ocean, not far away yet unseen from this distance.

I am unprepared for the scene outside. It is daylight again, the sky is blue, and no clouds interrupt the pure color. The area is still wide open and breezy, but the rolling hills have been replaced. I shield my eyes as they are stung by sparkles of light fluttering in the horizon, blinding me briefly. I close my eyes and can still see them, dancing on my retinas in bright flashes. I open my eyes slowly, adjusting them to the brightness of the scene in front of me. At first, I don't yet understand what is it that I am looking at. I see water, rectangles of water with thin walls between them. Are these pools? My sight clears some more. There is movement in the water, splashes and bubbles and tremendous commotion. Fish. The water pools are filled with fish. They swim in packed groups, bumping into each other in the overcrowded ponds, making ripples in the water where their spines break the surface. Some daring fish jump up and, for a second, are out of the water. Speckles of sunlight reflect off their slimy bodies and the surface.

I spot Nir ahead of me, hurrying on a narrow concrete path that divides the pools like a catwalk. I start after him as fast as I can. I had given up on calling his name, knowing he is not running away from me. He is leading me, and I follow. I need to figure out how to make him listen to me, as all my efforts so far failed. But for now, I just follow.

The sun is hot and blazing above our heads, I am sweaty, and my throat is parched. The abundance of water all around me makes it worse. I stop to catch my breath. Nir is still on the move. He is within my view, and I know where to look for him. I close my eyes and wait for my pulse to calm down.

When I open my eyes, everything goes black. I can't remember where I am or how I got here. The small of my back screams as I straighten up. The hair on my nape prickles as a whiff of wind breezes around me.

Nir. He was right next to me. He had a crab in his hand. He was leading me. I panic as it all rushes back in. *Did I miss him?* I turn my head in the direction I last saw him and see him in the distance, recognizable by his white shirt and striped pants. He is waiting for me, just beyond the fishponds.

I start again with new energy, walking quickly. As I push forward, the large pools become smaller in size, the fish in them less abundant. Closer to Nir, they are not pools anymore but large bathtubs, sunken in the ground, rows and rows of white porcelain tubs. These have one giant fish in each: dark gray carps, swimming aimlessly in clear water. Their mouths droop, tentacles extended at their corners.

When I reach the last one, I notice Nir has a basket at his feet filled with carp. They lie still, but I don't think they are dead. An eerie feeling fills me; they are waiting patiently to see what will happen to them. Then, as if to confirm my thought, a couple of them try breathing out of the water, opening and closing their mouths. When I am close enough, Nir picks up the basket and carries it on his back. He starts walking fast on the widening path.

He doesn't look back to check if I am following. A live fence made of lush green bushes lines the horizon. It is tall, the tallest hedge I've ever seen. Nir heads directly toward it. A narrow gap, barely visible, tore at the hedge. He steps sideways through the opening.

I reach the hedge and go through the gap. Both ends of the fence, growing on either side of the opening, are not aligned but rather overlap each other. This way the entrance is concealed and is hard to spot.

The grounds beyond are very familiar, yet I am unsure where I am. A narrow road stretches parallel to the tall green fence, with a row of eucalyptuses on the opposite side. A long building, two stories high, stands behind the trees, lined with open balconies and glass windows on both levels. Nir turns around a corner, into a walkway engulfing the building. I follow him to encircle its narrow side. The front is revealed, with a large expanse of green grass, cut to a perfect length. I sneeze as particles from the fresh cut grass hover in the air and penetrate my nose. I wipe my eyes with the back of my sleeve, and when they clear, it finally registers.

I am at the dormitory at Har Tzvi, the *yeshiva* the boys attended during their high school years. It's been several years since Nir graduated, but it looks exactly the same, although it is in the wrong location. I do not know where we are on the map—*if* there is one for this place.

Nir goes directly to the main entrance; it has no doors, just another wide gap in the wall, designed to allow hordes of all-male students to flow in and out quickly on their way to service prayers early in the morning or back at night after the evening meal. Right now, it is deserted.

From this side of the building, standing at its portal, I hear music coming from one of the rooms. Electric guitars and drums; someone sings in English.

I feel far away. Is there a way back home from here? A nagging thought at the back of my head tells me there is a way, but I can't remember what it is. It doesn't matter. All I want is to be with Nir, to save him. So I press on, into the dorms.

The building is divided into two wings; the entrance is positioned in the middle. Nir turns to the left wing, the carp basket in his hands. He lowers it down, and as he goes down the corridor, he stops by each room, takes a fish out of the basket, and places it at the door. On its long end, across from the rooms, the corridor has windowless openings. Wet towels hang on their sills to dry. The gentle sun sends warm rays, lightning Nir's face and illuminating the fish's scales, their hidden colors flickering. Some of the doors to the rooms are open.

Nir continues this strange ritual, distributing fish to each of the rooms, laying them down gently on the floor. I don't ask myself what to do next. I follow him.

I wander through the long corridor. Two rooms are closed shut. The carps Nir put on the floor are so eerie that the saying, "like fish out of water," comes to mind. Is Nir trying to tell me something with this strange ritual? One fish is missing an eye, a black hole glaring at me. The other fish's scales had started falling off and spreading on the floor. The door of the third room is open, so I peek in, avoiding stepping on the fish. This one lies upright on its belly, as if it were swimming and stopped in mid stroke.

Inside, the room is long and narrow. It has four beds, two on each side, a short bedding cupboard between them. Two elongated closets flank the doorway on each side. Everything is simple and utilitarian. At the far end, a closed balcony is extended out from the building. It has two desks with two chairs tucked under each. Through the clear glass, I can see the line of trees and the road they shade. Farther along is the green hedge.

The room looks just like I remember. Sarah was still alive, and we visited Ram and, later, Nir. I can't tell which room would have been Nir's. This room is bare and empty. It smells faintly of bleach and dust. The beds are unmade, the thin gray foam mattresses plainly showing their humble selves.

The walls are bare, the only embellishments are diagonally pasted pieces of yellowing tape.

I continue down the corridor, expecting to see more of the same—closed rooms or empty ones. When I reach the next open door, I am surprised to see that the room is not empty. Three boys sit on the bed to my right, playing a game of cards. A fourth boy sleeps on the opposite side.

I skip over the large fish by the door, and I step into the room. The boys don't seem to notice me. They continue playing their game while I stand in front of them. Can't they see me?

"*Shalom*," I say. The boys ignore me.

"*Shalom!*" I try again louder. I hear myself, but the boys don't seem to hear. They keep ignoring me, their heads together and focused on the cards.

Leaving the room, I start running in the corridor, calling Nir's name. "Nir, where are you? What is happening?"

I cannot find him, but there is an ugly fish at the entrance to each room, like a twisted trail of breadcrumbs. At the corridor's end, a sign marks the showers and bathrooms on one side. On its opposite, a flight of stairs leads upstairs. While I run, I glance inside the open rooms. There are more boys in them. Some are studying, their heads buried in large stacks of books on their desks. A couple of boys are fighting on the floor between the beds, pinning each other in a deadlock using hands, legs, and shoulders. Their friends cheer this name or that, not trying to break up the fight but encouraging it further. In one room several boys are smoking cigarettes. I don't stop at any of these rooms. I'm too afraid I won't see Nir, that I have lost him again.

I climb the stairs, wishing I could have climbed it two at a time, that I would have been in a better shape to sprint up a plain flight of steps. But I am not. By the time I reach the top floor I pant heavily. I am relieved to see the fish at the doors. That means only one thing. So I keep moving, this time along the corridor of the second floor, going back to the center of the building.

I notice movement in one of the rooms. Two tall boys are holding a third one, much smaller. He wears a blue *dubon*, a duvet winter coat that makes him look large and puffy, like a teddy bear—a *dooby*. All three have their backs to me. The one on the right, a red head—*Gingy*—holds Dooby's right arm, and on the left, a chubby boy with a severe case of acne pulls Dooby's coat sleeve.

"Leave me alone," Dooby says.

"Or what? What exactly will you do?" Gingy challenges him.

Dooby bites his lip, looking around frantically, searching for help. "I will go to Rabbi Tzvi. He will expel you."

"*Schtinker.* That's what you are, aren't you?" Acne Face says. "We will show you what happens to tattletales, stinky *schtinker.*" His face is inches from Dooby's, his eyes fierce. "No one will snitch on us and live to tell the tale after we are done with him!"

Dooby wriggles and tries to set himself loose from their grip. The two boys are stronger than him. Holding him on both sides, they drag him on the floor across the room and into the back balcony. Using his free hand, Gingy slides the window wide open. Next, they pick Dooby between them. When he is off the floor, still struggling to get loose and run away, Gingy picks up Dooby's legs while Acne tightly holds his upper body. They laugh, a rolling carefree head-jerking laugh. Dooby is not a challenge for them. Gingy rolls Dooby's feet beyond the railing.

I can't believe what I see. The older boys are about to drop the little one over the balcony! They are laughing, letting Dooby's feet dangle down, his legs kicking and jerking in the air, trying to find a hold. Dooby screams, begging them to pick him up and let him go.

"I won't tell anyone! I promise! Please let me up! I am going to fall! Please, guys, please! I am not a *schtinker*! I will not tell anyone!"

I am horrified that two religious boys, with *kippahs* on their heads and *tzitzit* tassels peeking from under their shirts, would bully their friend in such a way. Where did they learn to be so mean to other kids? Who are their parents who should have taught them *Ve'ahavta Lere'acha Kmocha*? And you shall love your friend as you love yourself!

I rush to them. With both hands, I reach to grab hold of their collars. My mouth opens instinctively in a shout, "Stop it right now!"

Just like before, the boys seem not to hear me. And my hands, instead of getting a hold on their shirts, go through their bodies as if they were thin air, a hallucination. *But they are right here in front of my eyes, and I can hear them and see Dooby's tears and...* There is nothing I can do to save him.

Dooby wriggles some more, screaming for them to stop and lift him back to safety. Suddenly, both of his hands slip through the thick coat's sleeves. He falls to the ground with a thud.

"No!" I shout. The scream echoes in my head.

Gingy and Acne hold the coat like a dead goat. They freeze, both looking at the empty shell in their hands, expecting to see Dooby in it. Then, in slow motion, they look at each other, rise on the ball of their feet, and look down to see where Dooby landed.

"Shit!" they shout in unison and dart back through the room, out the door, and down the stairs. In their haste, they drop Dooby's coat at my feet.

The small boy is lying on the ground below the balcony. He is moaning, a good sign. He may have broken a few bones from the fall, but he is conscious. I wait several seconds, just enough to see the two older boys downstairs. They dash from around the building to where Dooby is lying. Good. At least they have the decency to help him rather than scurry away like scared little crabs hiding in their burrows.

A thick lump rises from my stomach into my throat, gastric acid burns my airways. I sit on the first bed I can reach, clenching my belly with both hands. My entire body spasms in aggressive waves. Cold sweat engulfs me. I must continue, so I rise to my feet, and they almost crash under me. As soon as I stabilize myself upright I leave the room and follow the fish trail.

At the center of the building, past the staircase, the corridor continues on the opposite wing. The sun descends toward Earth, casting its long warm hands on the doors lining the hallway. A stench fills my nostrils: the smell of deserted beaches where dead fish are washed to shore, their stinking flesh a feast to feisty seagulls. Like the first dorm wing, most of the rooms here are occupied by teenage boys, engaged in different pastimes—praying, studying, eating, bullying, drinking beer, or fighting.

I avert my eyes away. What good would it do now? I can't control what these boys are doing anyway, God is my witness that I have tried. But I wonder, was this how my boys' friends behaved? *Was this how Ram and Nir behaved?* Did they act like this and I was clueless? No, not my boys. They were good boys, serious and mature. They would know what is right and what is wrong, and most of what I saw is very wrong!

I hurry down the long corridor, avoiding the other rooms. I just want to move on.

That's when I see the fish at the door to the shower room.

***

The door is slightly open, light seeping through the gap. Heavy steam spills out with the light, like smoke coming out of a burning room. It engulfs the dead fish as it emerges.

I stop at the door, waiting for something to happen, anything. Should I move on or check what's inside? Throughout the previous corridor, I skipped over the closed doors and did not bother opening them to see what was inside. The open rooms were disturbing enough, horrifying even. Here the door is not shut closed nor wide open. As if sensing my hesitation, it starts opening slightly, thicker fumes and light pushing its way out. Can the steam push the door open? I step aside to let whoever is on the other side come through. There must be someone there!

Nothing happens. I don't want to touch the door with my bare hands. Its beige Formica surface has started to separate at the edges. Several bumps and bubbles formed around the metal handle. They seem to breathe, growing and shrinking in size. I rub my eyes with my palms to clear them, and when I open them again I hope to see the door in its normal state, but it's not. If anything, the lumps in the Formica grew in number and spread in a large fan shape toward the hinges. Condensation drips in long narrow columns from the top of the door.

I find a clear spot in the middle of the door and push it lightly with my elbow; just a small nudge, really.

The door reacts to my touch as if I hit it with a truck head on; it swings inward swiftly, then abruptly stops midway as a loud scratching noise comes from its other side, and the door springs back my way. Now I feel the force that pulls me from within. I must find out what made that noise. Without a second thought, I shove both hands at the same clear spot, now wet and slimy. I am relieved that I used enough force and the door pushes whatever is behind it, clearing the path to open all the way through. I won't have to touch it again.

I step inside. Behind the door, a long wooden bench is lying diagonally on its side, two of its legs hidden from view. Several towels, clothing articles, toiletry bags, soap bars, and shampoo bottles are spread around it in disarray. The bench was there to block the door, not being too successful in that role.

The changing room is large. A row of sinks and mirrors lines one wall. Benches stand flushed against the other walls. Metal hooks hang above them, towels draping off two of them. A pair of *tzitzit* and more clothes are folded neatly on one of the benches. I see the source of the fog; an opening in one of the walls marks the way to the communal showers. I hear the water running. The wet heavy air smells like fresh pines.

On one of the mirrors, someone finger-sketched in the steam; a heart with a piercing arrow, one end pointing to a single letter—a *Nun.* Another letter floats on the other side—an *Aleph.* The entire crude message is covered with a new layer of condensation, water beads pulled to the earth by their weight.

I don't hesitate anymore and run inside without thinking, I want to see who is in the shower. When I reach the showers the steam envelops me. It is hard to breathe. Sweat pours heavily from my forehead and behind my ears. Salt stings my eyes.

Two boys are in the showers. They are naked, and hot water runs from two showerheads. The stalls have no dividers, no curtains. The boys are hugging, thrusting into each other. The one with his back to me has his face at the nook of his friend's neck. The leg of his accomplice is wrapped around the first boy's body, his face pointing toward the ceiling, his eyes closed. He thrusts and grinds, his movements fast, desperate.

I stumble backward, my stomach heavy, my heart pounding fast. My eyes burn, not from the heat and steam, but from the obscene act in front of me.

Then I see the hair. The boy with his back to me—his hair. It is Nir's hair. Brown, long, smooth. The water runs over his head, it straightens and lengthens the strands on his nape, splits and re-splits his hair as the stream changes its course. But it can't be Nir! Nir had a woman. It's hard for me to think of her, of Nir being with her, but she *was* a woman. So what is this? It can't be Nir.

In seconds, their act is over. The two boys climax, then their bodies fall loose, quickly detached from each other.

"We cannot do this ever again," the boy with Nir's hair says. He pushes himself away from his friend to wash away his shame.

The knot tightens deep in my stomach; it wrenches me from within. I stumble back, hurrying through the large dressing room. I avoid looking at the mirrors and the vulgar graffiti. The floor is wet, and I must be careful not to slip. My eyes sting. I rub them hard; tears mixing in with my sweat. A dead fish stench attacks my nostrils, swallowing the soap smell. That damn fish! I lean on the wall, my head low between my knees. I take several deep breaths in an attempt to stop the nausea. I open my eyes and see the fish is between my feet. Its head is smashed, the eye socket caved in and that entire side of the head twisted and flat. The tongue protrudes from its mouth cavity, squeezed out with the same force that flattened the head. Did I step on it on my way out?

Was it Nir? I only saw his back. The hair... it was just like Nir's...

In all the years Ram and Nir attended the *yeshiva*, it never crossed my mind that these abominations happened here. Would I have sent them here had I known? No. A thousand percent no.

But the voice... It was not Nir's voice. Another boy. It was not my Nir. I am sure of that.

My heart slows down, and I breathe better. My stomach has quieted down as well.

And even if it was his voice (but it wasn't!), this happened at least four or five years ago. Since then, Nir has had a girlfriend, a woman!

I must get away from this place. I run down the stairs, putting some distance between myself and these boys. I want to find Nir again. I *need* to find him! I know he is somewhere waiting for me.

The stairs take me back to the lower level, on the eastern end of the dorm building. I walk back toward the main entrance. I can see Nir. He sits on the floor cross-legged in front of one of the rooms. The basket is perched on the floor next to him. I can't see if he has more fish in it, but there are none on the floor at the door in front of him. I approach closer. The door is open. Nir stares inside, rocking his upper body back and forth. He doesn't notice me.

I am going to speak with him now, no matter what! All my previous tries have failed. I will not give up. I reach slowly and stand next to him. He doesn't stir, just sits there, rocking and staring in front of him. I sit on the floor half a meter away from him. I can't risk scaring him away. I am so close now that I could stretch my hands to touch him if I wanted to. Back and forth his upper body rocks, his hands hugging his shoulders, his gaze fixated inside the room.

"Nir," I try. "Nir, please. If you can talk, please say something."

Nothing. Rocking back and forth, his arms unfold their shoulders hug, he raises them toward his long hair. He starts fidgeting with strands of hair, pulling lightly.

"Nir, it has been so long, and I missed you. I am so happy to see you. I want to talk to you. It's not too late. I can help you. Please look at me and tell me something."

Nothing. Rocking in place. Fidgeting with his hair. Eyes on their target.

"Since Imma died things have not been the same… It has been so hard! Please, Niri. I am begging you."

Nir turns his head slowly to the right. Finally! He looks briefly at a space above me. He then lowers his gaze and looks directly at me—no, not at me but through me. A single teardrop falls from his eye and runs down his face. Its trail follows the curve of his cheek and the corner of his mouth.

He keeps his gaze on me for a few seconds. It feels like an eternity. He then turns it again and looks at the open room.

Frustrated, I want to jump on my feet and hold him with both hands and shake him. I want to shout in his face and make him hear me. I want him to listen! Instead, I follow his gaze, looking inside the room.

What is it that I see right in front of me? I squint my eyes, trying harder to make sense of what it is. But nothing makes sense anymore.

The room looks bigger than all the other rooms, deeper, like a huge hall with cathedral ceiling and expanse of space, the far corners dark, engulfed in shadows. At the same time, the room looks smaller, crowded to its rims like an over-crowded synagogue on the high holidays. It is filled up with airplane models everywhere. Toy aircraft replicas of every variety, size and color. Small ones like those coming in chocolate eggs. Large ones, like hobbyists fly around on the sand hills by the ocean. There are plastic models, others made of metal assembled with bolts and screws, Papier-mâché, even spaghetti ones. They are painstakingly painted and decorated with decals to look like real airplanes—warplanes, jets, American planes, Israeli fighters, passenger airliners, single pilot planes. They hang from the ceiling in various flying positions, suspended by clear fishing lines. They cling to the walls, covering every available spot. Several remote-controlled models are flying around, rising, diving, twisting, and turning. One of them billows a double-streak of cloudy trail behind it, and each has a unique engine sound. Hundreds of models are scattered on the floor, covering it completely, so thick in places that they lean on each other, like fallen domino pieces.

In the middle of the room, between the chaos of wings, wheels, and propellers, sits another Nir.

CHAPTER 7

Tuesday, Third Day of the Shiva

RAM

"Today?" Ram's voice pitched as he turned to look at Baruch. "What are you talking about?" Chaim mentioned Nir last night after he fainted, but his father was confused and disoriented. Now he is talking about seeing Nir?

A new wave of onion stench hit Ram from Baruch's breath as he explained, "We were sitting and chatting, and he seems to be, well, happy. In the beginning we didn't talk about Nir, so I thought he was just glad to be distracted and talk about other things. You know, the soccer league and the Euro-league, stuff like that. We even talked politics, and he got excited about Bibi's upcoming congress speech. You know how he can sometimes be, right?" Baruch's eyes bulged, and his hand brushed his comb-over again.

"And? What about Nir?" Ram wanted Baruch to get to the point.

"Yes, yes. When we started encouraging Chaim to talk about Nir, instead of the somberness you would expect, he became even more cheerful! He said that he saw him, yesterday *and* today!" Baruch shook his head, leaning closer to Ram.

Ram rolled his eyes. He didn't know whether he should encourage Baruch to tell him more, or just ignore this nonsense.

"It's quite common," Baruch insisted. "Grief-stricken people talk about the dead as if they were still alive, out of habit. Sometimes they even have fantasies that their lost ones are back." He took a quick glance over his shoulder, and then back to Ram, shifting his chair under him so that he faced Ram almost squarely. "Do you know Leah?" he nodded his head backward, one of his eyebrows raised.

"Mrs. Schwartz?" Ram looked at that direction, then back at Baruch.

"Yes, Leah Schwartz. Well, when her father passed away, may his memory be blessed, her mother was still alive. She died two or three years ago, I think. No, maybe four years…"

Ram fidgeted in his seat. "What does that have to do with—"

"Yes, yes," Baruch interrupted. "So, when her father passed away, her mother would set the table for him, plate and silverware, glass and food and everything, and she would make him his tea and wait for him to come back from the synagogue, and she would talk to him all day long, as if he was still alive and right there…"

"How old was she? Ninety?"

"Oh, not ninety, maybe in her late eighties. I can ask Leah." Baruch started turning around.

"She was either senile or in shock," Ram raised his voice. He didn't need Baruch to start checking around how old Mrs. Schwartz's mother was. It was utterly irrelevant. "Abba is probably in shock himself!"

Baruch's attention was back on him. "Your Abba…" He shook his head. "It's different. He doesn't look in shock! No, he is, eh—" he searched for the word, then decided on one, "—happy. He behaves like a happy person."

"He *is* in shock!" Ram almost shouted.

Silence fell in the room. The people around them looked at Ram, their conversations paused mid-sentence. Ram lowered his voice to a whisper. "Do you think he knows what he is talking about, after everything that he has gone through in the past few years?"

"I don't know what is causing this," Baruch said. "All I know is that he needs to grieve and get it out of his system, and this fantasy won't help."

Ram took a deep breath. He had to calm down to make sense of the situation. "What did he say, exactly?"

"Well, let me see… He talked about seeing Nir on the beach, and Nir was playing, building sandcastles. Then they walked together, and they saw an old synagogue, Ashlag I think, and they learned together. More stuff like that. It didn't make much sense, but he was so convinced it just happened." Baruch raised his head, his eyes wide. "Maybe it's a dream your dad had! Do you know how he sleeps?"

Ram wasn't sure. Last night Dr. Frisch gave Chaim some sleeping pills. He might have dreamt about Nir under the drug's effect. It sounds like the most logical explanation.

"Yes, that's probably it," Ram said. He had heard enough of that nonsense and wanted to see for himself what Chaim was babbling about. With that, he turned his attention back to the other people in the room. Sometime during their discussion, Chaim left his room and returned to the place he so enjoyed, being the center of attention. He was in the middle of another story, owning the entire audience . While he talked, his animated hands pierced the air, illustrating some of his points.

"He *loved* his airplanes. He would watch that air force movie again and again. What was it called?" Chaim glared at the air above them, searching.

"*Top Gun*," Ram helped him.

"Yes, yes, *Top Gun*, that's it! I am telling you, he knew the entire dialogue by heart. He didn't care much about the love story; it was always about the jet fighters. He would sit on the sofa as if inside an F-16s' cockpit, jerking his hands here and there, citing the lines with the actors on the—"

"F-14," Ram said.

"What?" Chaim looked as if he was surprised to see Ram.

"F-14. *Top Gun* had F-14s, not F-16s."

"F-14, F-16, what's the difference?" Chaim laughed and caught his breath again to continue his story.

Ram didn't push. You couldn't grow up with Nir not knowing about his passion for airplanes, especially war jets. His dream was to become an air force pilot. At times, that was all he talked about. But Ram was not surprised his father didn't know the difference between an F-14 and F-16. And what would be the point now to insist on this detail?

"Did you know how good he was at building airplane models?" Chaim asked his friends. They nodded, agreeing to every word. "Whenever someone asked him what he wanted for his birthday, it was a new airplane kit. He spent hours in his room building them. They have so many small parts, and the instructions are very complicated. He had so much patience with them," Chaim reflected. "And he didn't like using the decals they came with, those that stick on to decorate the planes. He preferred painting them on his own. He had such a good steady hand."

At this Ram *was* surprised. His father never paid much attention to their hobbies. On the contrary, Chaim believed that these pastimes were a way to kill time and not learn anything new. He despised video games and never hid his distaste of their friends who spent their time playing them. As for watching TV, he canceled the cables service after their mother died, claiming there was nothing to watch anyway, keeping the aging television set and its rabbit ears antenna only for the news, which he religiously watched every weeknight.

"Abba, you didn't like him building them! It was Imma who encouraged him, and you always said he was spoiled." Ram said it so fast, he didn't realize he had said it out loud. "Oh, Abba, I'm so—"

"I know," Chaim cut him, his gaze drifted to his palms, now resting in his lap like two dead fish. "He loved it so much," Chaim continued, "and I am glad that your mother didn't listen to me."

Ram was speechless. Did he just hear his father admitting he was wrong?

***

He remembered the last fight his parents had about Nir's airplane models. He was about twelve at the time, reading in the boys' bedroom, the room he shared with Nir since he could remember. An extended balcony stretched the length of the apartment along their parents' master bedroom, the boys' room, and the living room. The door to the balcony was open in hope that some breeze would find its way into the hot rooms and through to the other end of the house.

Ram lay on his stomach on the bed, the open book down on the floor below him. He was oblivious to the chaos around him, a typical boys' room—the desks overflowed with notebooks, papers, board games, pens and crayons, stacks of cassettes, cards, and other odd items only boys find interesting. Above the desk, shelves were loaded with books, somewhat organized by size and subject. The two swiveling chairs were completely hidden under piles of clothes, and the floor was covered with socks and shoes. Nir's blanket was spread on the floor around the bed, and on the opposite wall the doors of the wardrobe were ajar.

"You are spoiling him," he suddenly heard his father say. His voice was loud and agitated, breaking Ram's attention from the book. "There are better ways we can spend our money, and there are better ways he can spend his time!"

"This is not spoiling," came his mother's voice, determined. "Did you ever look at him when he builds them? He is *happy*. He forgets about the sadness and depression, and he is just happy. He is a kid. Let him be."

"This is all your fault, the depression and psychology mumbo jumbo. He is fine. All he needs is decent discipline. If the times were different, if it were *my* father's time, he would have already been feeling the backside of my belt."

"Never!" It was Sarah's turn to raise her voice, as protective as a lioness shielding her cubs. "The second you do that, we are over. I will take the children, and you will never see them again!" Ram could imagine how she looked at that moment—her eyes bulging, energy shooting in his direction. He seldom witnessed them fighting, but when they did, he knew his mother was not a woman who said "Amen" to everything her husband said, and when it came to her children no one could cross her, including his father.

"Of course I will not. It was just a figure of speech," Chaim tried to appease her. "You know I would never raise my hand to the kids." She did. "But I still think you are overprotective. There is nothing wrong with him. He needs to go out, play ball with his friends. Maybe moving him to another school will help."

Ram was glad Nir was not there to hear them. He didn't plan on telling him, either. Their mother usually prevailed, so what would be the point? He looked fondly at the collection of airplane models that had already accumulated in their room, all built by Nir. The one spotless and organized place in the room was the first two shelves above Nir's desk where he displayed his airplanes, organized and reorganized in different formations. Ram liked looking at them but had no patience to build them. When they got their first model, he immediately gave up on constructing it, leaving the entire project for Nir, who hadn't stopped since.

The next day, when he returned from school, his mother was in the kitchen. She didn't greet him with her usual happy smile and questions about his day. Her eyes were red, and she hid a crumpled tissue paper in her palm.

"What happened, Imma? Are you crying?" he asked. As he hugged her, she put her head on his, sniffling.

"It's Nir. He broke all of them. I don't know why," her voice shook.

"Broke what?" Ram didn't follow her.

"His airplanes." She sat heavily in one of the kitchen's chairs while Ram darted to the room.

They were all there, but not even one was whole. It looked like an enemy fleet came in the dead of night and bombed them all. Bits and pieces were scattered on the floor on top of abandoned clothes and socks and inside shoes, on the shelves, on the beds and desks, covering the books and papers, boxes and cassettes. They were broken, their decals shredded to bits. Small heaps of wings, wheels, propellers.

Why would Nir do something like that? Nir loved them—loved to build them. But even more, he loved organizing them on the shelves, arranging them by size or era, manufacturers or type.

Sarah came into the room, a broom and duster in her hands. "Come. Help me," she said.

They worked quietly, collecting the smashed pieces, packing hours upon hours of Nir's hard work and dedication into one black garbage bag.

"When did he do it?" Ram wondered, "And *why*?"

"I don't know why. He won't tell me. He ran off to play with a friend when I came home. He was already back from school, and he dropped his school bag on the kitchen floor. I brought it here and found this."

Ram thought about his parent's argument from the previous night. Where was Nir? Could he have heard them?

It was the last time Nir played with any airplane model. The next time their mother bought him a new model, he refused to take it. He didn't want to build any more airplanes, he said. He was too old for it, he said. With it, Nir lost the sparkle in his eyes, the way they shined when he hunched over his latest project, concentrating on the details, blocking out the rest of the world. No one has ever again seen him admire his creations, proudly displaying them for everyone to see.

***

"Now you are saying this?" Ram said, not caring who will hear him. "You never liked him building them. He destroyed all his airplanes because of you!"

Tears welled in Chaim's eyes. "You don't understand," he said. "I saw Nir. He showed me his collection. He built so many of them. Thousands of airplanes. He never stopped. They were all there, the first one and each one he got after. He also built them from parts and materials he found. Some had real engines and remote controls. They were flying around…"

"What are you talking about, Abba? Where did you see him? He never built models since that day when he broke all of them, not here, not anywhere."

"You won't understand," Chaim insisted, his head still down. Ram strained his ears to hear. "Since that man came here yesterday, I have seen Nir. He takes me places, shows me things."

"Abba, you need to rest. You are not making any sense." Ram frowned, his distress now fueled by a concern for Chaim's mental health. He looked around at his father's friends. The looks on their faces varied between pity, compassion, incredulity, surprise, and awe. Most of them were quiet, nodding their heads in agreement.

Mrs. Schwartz fidgeted in her chair. She looked around with her mouth open. She seemed like a child worrying if what she would say would be appropriate or not, hoping that someone else would say it before her. Then, she made up her mind.

"Chaim, you must be in shock, please—"

"I don't need to rest!" Chaim insisted. "I am not tired, and I am not crazy." He looked at all of them. "This stranger—I wish I knew who he was. He touched me, and he gave me a gift. I can see Nir, and I am telling you, I am getting to know him now." And quietly he added, "And I think I can save him."

Ram thought he didn't hear clearly. *Save him? Save Nir? This has gone too far!* He slumped back on the sofa, feeling deflated and depressed.

One by one, Chaim's friends rose to their feet. "We have to go," said one. His wife stood on his toes, rearranging the strap of her purse on her shoulder.

"Yes, we should get going too. We have some tickets for the theater tonight," said another.

Mrs. Schwartz leaned forward in her chair, and put a comforting hand on Chaim's arm. She was gentle and warm.

"You have suffered a great loss, Chaim. Please take care of yourself. I brought some food. Chava put it in the refrigerator. I hope you will like it. It's my special zucchini and onion quiche. I also brought some fresh fruit."

Then she turned to look at Ram. "You too, Rami." She always called him Rami, a nickname he abandoned years ago. "Please take care of Abba." She leaned closer to him, and in a lower tone she added, "Call me at any time, Rami. I know what you must be going through. And your father needs professional help." She lowered her voice further. "I know someone who can help him. I can give you his number."

With that, she rose to her feet and left, her husband trailing behind.

***

TAMMY

Tammy didn't follow the entire discussion between Chaim, his circle of friends, and Ram. She observed them from the outskirts of the living room, sitting quietly like a single audience member watching the theater unfolding in front of her.

Chaim made a peculiar impression on her. Not what she expected, that's for sure. The picture she had in her mind was based solely on Ram's attitude and body language whenever he talked about his father. She expected a large, heavy set man, tall and robust, with defined features, personality rather than age wrinkles framing cold eyes, which are always stern and void of any humor. In fact, she imagined him to be just like General Saban who visited their base every Wednesday, making it the most hated day of the week for her and her staff.

What she saw now was a man surrounded by many friends. He was shorter than Ram by three centimeters and wider around his midsection. Nothing in him was sharp and defined. His hairline, though still quite full, didn't seem to start or end in a specific spot, but rather clung to his forehead and sideburns in uneven patches of gray and black hair. His eyes were soft and heavy, the skin under them pulled back toward his jaw. His clothes, two sizes too big, hung off his body. The shirt was tucked into his pants in folds, and the tight belt completed the crumpled look below. His appearance did not seem to matter for him.

When his friends surrounded him, he was animated, his entire body talking with him. And Tammy saw something else in his eyes. While his friends were around, his eyes took everything and everyone in, and in turn, Chaim gave attention to each one of them. But when the friends left one by one, the light in his eyes faded, one person at a time. Now he sat alone, those lively eyes half closed and barren, his entire body defeated. Finally, his heavy head lolled to one side, soft snores punctuating the rise and fall of his stomach.

In another corner of the large living room, by the dining nook, Tammy saw Millie. The stark difference between her dark hair and her china pale complexion gave her a ghostly aura. It was intensified by her somber expression and the old prayer book, constantly in her hands like a permanent extension.

Tammy rose to join her at the oval table. She pulled an abandoned chair and sat across from Millie. It took Millie several seconds to realize someone had joined her. Her head was down in her prayer book, her mouth chanting quietly. When she finally sensed the intrusion, she looked up at her. Tammy did not like what she saw in that first instant. She saw fear and hate and a calculating mind thinking how to run away.

"Please, stay," Tammy said. "I don't bite."

Millie already clutched the prayer book close to her heart and started to push herself up off the chair.

"Please," Tammy reached closer. "I know what it feels to lose a loved one."

"You know nothing!" Millie hissed, not looking at her.

"I do." Tammy stayed calm. "And Ram—" She wanted to say how much Ram was worried about her and their father. She wanted to tell her how worried she was for them. But at the mention of her brother, Millie's head jerked up, her eyes emitting the same emotions Tammy had seen before, condensed with pure hate.

"You! It's because of *you* that Ram is not coming home anymore. And it's because of *you* that he doesn't wear his *kippah* and is not religious anymore!" Tears rolled easily from Millie's eyes.

Oh, poor girl. If she only knew. If anything, Tammy encouraged Ram to keep some of his traditions, for his family's sake and his own peace of mind. She strongly believed in "live and let live" and wanted him to make his own decisions about what to believe in and what to reject.

"You are wrong." She shook her head, looking straight into Millie's eyes. "Ram is a grown man and can make his own decisions. He—"

But Millie refused to listen. She pushed her chair back. It slammed the wall behind her. She ran away toward the bedrooms.

Tammy sighed. She realized it was a mistake to reach out to Millie. What was she thinking? Millie needed an adult female to lean onto. But someone who would understand her, understand where she is coming from. They had nothing in common, other than Ram. And Millie saw her as the woman who took him away from them. So how could she be of any help?

Tammy needed to see Ram. She looked around but didn't see him in the living room. She peeked into the kitchen and found it was empty. She tried for his room. She knocked gently on the door and went in. Ram was lying on his bed, a yellowish tennis ball in his hand. He threw it in the air, caught it in one hand, then threw it up again.

"He is going crazy," he said without looking at her. She knew he was talking about his father.

Tammy sat at the edge of the bed. "Not crazy," she said. "Confused."

Ram contemplated what she said. He kept throwing the ball. "Maybe *I* will go crazy eventually. A few more days in this place... I can't wait for this *shiva* to be over."

"It's your time to grieve as much as his, and everyone has their way to mourn." She put a gentle hand on his shoulder. He looked at her. "Just be patient with him. It will pass, and things will be normal again; as normal as they can be."

"At least I don't live here anymore, and I have no plans to come back. But Millie is still here. I don't know what will happen with her."

"Things will somehow find a way to improve. You'll see." She didn't mention Millie's outburst. There will be time for that.

"Like they did for Nir?" He looked back at the ceiling, throwing the ball again. And again.

CHAPTER 8

Nir is inside the room.

Nir is outside of the room.

I look at Nir inside the room. Even from my vantage point, the room feels claustrophobic, with Nir surrounded by the chaos of toy airplane models. My gaze moves to the other Nir, sitting right next to me at the door, outside the room. They are looking at each other. Nir inside is a younger version. His face is smooth, clear of any facial hair. His hair is cut short, parted on one side neatly. A small airplane cradles in his lap, about thirty centimeters long and twice as much in wingspan. I recognize it. It's the first model he ever built. Sarah's mother gave it to the boys as a gift from America when she returned from one of her trips. Something is not right with it—it seems to be glued together from bits and pieces, hairline cracks crisscrossing in odd ways around its entire structure as if it was excavated and reconstructed by an archeologist in an ancient mound.

Suddenly, Nir, the one sitting next to me, the older Nir that I followed here, stands up. He starts pacing around in circles, his palms thrust into his temples, and his head jerks violently. He storms at the wall adjacent to the door, crushing his entire body in frustration. He makes a fist with his right hand and punches the wall, again and again.

I stand up. Younger Nir inside the room doesn't move, still nursing the precious toy in his hands. Without thinking, I reach for Nir, the one right next to me, the upset, wall-punching Nir. I touch his shoulder. He turns around to face me and shouts.

"No!"

Just once, his voice throaty and deep, like an animal hauling from the bottom of a bottomless pit. I stumble backward, holding my hands in front of me, not sure what to do next. Nir finally acknowledged me, talked to me. I want so much more, but I am scared and not sure how to proceed.

He stares at me, his eyes on fire, spit dripping from his mouth, his breath heavy, panting. He must have hurt his knuckles when attacking the wall, but his hands are clean, unharmed.

"Abba," younger Nir inside the room says, catching both of us by surprise.

We both turn our heads to look inside. Nir's younger self stands on his feet, his left hand stretched out, the airplane's nose pointing at our direction.

"Abba," he repeats.

He then starts moving forward, step by step. He seems to float through the small airplanes covering the floor. Even though the models hide his feet all the way above his ankles, they don't shuffle around, as if he walks in water, not toys.

I am frozen in place. I forget about the older Nir and his rage attack just seconds ago. The older Nir, who for the first time since I saw him at the beach, had acknowledged me. But all I see is my younger boy, his younger version, his handsome boyish face, smart eyes, inquiring mouth. Tears stream freely from my eyes.

My beautiful young boy continues walking toward me in the room until he reaches the door. He doesn't step outside the room, and his arm still stretched out, holding the airplane. He takes another small step, and the airplane crosses the invisible line between the room and the corridor. After a long moment, my young beautiful Nir nods to me, raising his outstretched hand higher. The airplane's nose is almost touching me. He wants me to have it.

I hold up my hands, my entire body is shaking. The little stone is in my right hand. I free two fingers, holding it tight with the rest. With seven outstretched fingers, I reach the airplane. It is warm to the touch. I close them on its wings, one hand on each side of its body.

Nir retracts his hand and smiles at me. So many years passed since I saw this smile. Maybe since he was a toddler. The one saying, "I am happy, I trust you, I love you." He then turns around, and faster than he came, he returns to the back of the room. He picks up another plane and starts playing with it, lifting it up in the air and sounding engine noises with his mouth.

A few minutes pass, maybe longer. I stand there at the open door to the oversized room, looking at the younger version of my son playing with his collection of airplanes, his first airplane still in my hands. My stomach, my guts, my heart—at that moment, at that eternity, I carry the world's weight inside me. So much lost time, the years I missed, not playing with him, not seeing him enjoying what he loved so much.

I shall tell him how sorry I am. I shall tell him how wrong I was. And I must warn him, tell him to stay away from the sea, save him. He stands right next to me, and I will tell him that.

I turn to face my son, the older Nir, the one who led me here. The corridor is empty. He is gone, and I panic.

What now? Where did he go?

***

There are no more fish at the entrances to the rest of the rooms down the hall. I rush by them, all the way to the main entrance, and leave the building. Darkness has fallen and engulfed this place. The vast expanse of clipped grass is now pitch black, a vast area of nothingness. A couple of tall streetlights stand in the dark, but they are not bright enough to illuminate the entire complex. I run on the path back the way we came. I don't see Nir anywhere. What should I do next? Should I continue and assume he would be there, or should I go back? Maybe there was another way out of the dorms? He might have gone again into the west wing of the building. Or did he go into one of the rooms?

I then hear a whistle, sharp and deafening. It comes from the direction ahead of me. I decide to follow the path. My gut instinct tells me I am on the right track. So far, Nir has made sure I won't lose him. I relax slightly. With the airplane in one hand and the little stone in the other, I continue walking, looking for any sign of my boy.

I walk this way for what feels like hours. Every time I get discouraged, when I think that I chose the wrong path, when I want to turn back or just sit down to rest, I hear that awful whistle. The sporadic streetlights irradiate the way, and the whistle encourages me to continue. The way I came from looks exactly like the way ahead—winding path marked by streetlights, darkness all around it. A sense of déjà vu engulfs me when I look both ways. I take a step forward and feel as if I go back the way I came. I have to make a decision and move. I can't stay here, so I continue where my gut tells me to go. The whistle keeps guiding me. I am disoriented and tired, but I can't stop now.

Finally, the road widens again. Rows of streetlights stretch in several directions, like straight tentacles of an enormous octopus. Yellow lines on the ground sketch gigantic prehistoric fishbones, neatly organized under the circle of lights. I arrived at an abandoned parking lot, and the road cuts through it right in the middle. It is very quiet, the air crisp and chilly. My body wants me to stop and rest, but I should not. I am too afraid to get confused and walk in the wrong direction. Is there a right direction anyway?

The lights in the distance change. They are colder—blues and whites—unlike the warm yellows and oranges of the parking lot around me. Smoke rises above these new lights. As I get closer, I see a bulky outline has shaped itself in the smoke: a building, the source of the lights and smoke. A tall chimney stack hovers behind it, spitting white smoke into the night sky. Light spills out through large windows. *Another building*, I can't stop thinking. Nir takes me to another building, this one cold and large and frightening in the middle of a moonless night, surrounded only by an empty parking lot.

I should know that building. Like the Ashlag synagogue and the *yeshiva* dorms, I should have known Nir took me to another building we both knew. Something in its shape feels familiar, the chimney, the rows of windows. I realize where I am when I arrive at its gate.

No, I cry quietly, desperately. *Not here, Nir. Please, just not here.*

CHAPTER 9

Tuesday, Third Day of the Shiva

RAM

Later that day, as Ram sat on the mourners' sofa with his father and Millie, just before *Mincha* time, a constant stream of people came through the door into the apartment. The place filled quickly, and people stood everywhere. The living room was packed, men squeezed body to body around the dining table, in the hallway to the bedrooms, in the kitchen. When there was no more space and the front door was blocked, they lined up outside the apartment, by the open door on the landing, and down the stairs. It was stuffy and hot. Someone slid open the large window panels to let in some air. Outside, the world was still. No breeze flowed through the tired buildings; no respite came into the packed apartment. The air inside, thick and ripe, filled with anticipation. Ram felt the tension but failed to understand what drew so many people in, like caged animals waiting for their feeding time.

Ram watched his father. Chaim sat erect in his place, his head turning in all directions. His right-hand fingers drummed on his jerking knee.

"Who are you looking for?" Ram asked.

Chaim ignored him, still looking around.

"Abba?" Ram asked, a bit sharply.

"That guy, from the other day," Chaim said, not stopping to look at Ram as he did.

"A—" Ram started. Then he changed his mind. *If he comes here again*, Ram thought, *I will take care of this nonsense, see what his real intentions are.* The child in him hoped that this insanity will pass on its own. If the mystery man wouldn't come back and his father wouldn't have any more episodes, things would go back to the way they were.

The way they were. Nothing would ever be the same. Another invisible rock fell into the depth of Ram's heart, weighing it down deeper.

Throughout *Mincha*, Chaim stood on his feet, searching. While they learned the daily *Mishnayot* after the service, more people squeezed into the apartment, which by now was full to the brim.

Ma'ariv was over. The mourners sat down on the low sofa, waiting for the line of consolers to form. Strangers looked at each other, waiting for something to happen. The neighbors from upstairs, the kiosk owner down the street, a couple of people who worked at Chaim's accounting firm—they all pushed their way through the crowd and lined up to say their goodbyes. All eyes observed the line of consolers as if they were waiting for something to happen.

Who are all of these people, and why aren't they going home? Ram looked at his father, who was oblivious to the bizarre situation. He resumed his earlier stance at the edge of the sofa, studying each person in the crowd, scanning their faces.

A stir in the crowd to their right caught Ram's attention. Asher Shalom pushed his way through from the direction of the door. His face was flushed, as if he stood for hours in the sun.

"What's going on?" Ram asked Asher Shalom when he reached them.

"Maybe you know more than I do," Asher Shalom replied. "Some people at the back are talking about a *Mekubal*, a Kabbalist who appeared here last night, and they want to see him."

"A *Mekubal*?" Ram shook his head. His father's expression stayed the same, scanning the crowd. Nothing indicated he had registered Asher Shalom's words.

"There are rumors about a holy man… He visits *shiva* houses around the country and blesses the mourners."

"Nonsense," Ram rolled his eyes.

Asher Shalom reached closer to Ram. He bent down so his face was just above Ram's and lowered his voice. "No one is sure exactly what he looks like or where he lives." He ignored Ram's doubtful reaction. "Some describe an ancient man, wrinkled and parched like an old leather shoe, with white hair and long white beard. Others are talking about a young Yemenite Rabbi, with black curly sidelocks, wearing a traditional long striped dress. I even heard a theory that this *Mekubal* is a descendant of King David because people swear he is a redhead!"

"And they," Ram gestured around, "think that this man had come here? *Will* come here again?"

Asher Shalom nodded.

"You know what I think?" Ram stood up. "That they are all *crazy!*" He looked at the crowd, raised his voice and said, "Please, everyone. Listen to me." He hated the tremble in his voice.

Hush fell over the room. Everyone looked at him.

"Please go home," he continued. "There was no *Mekubal* or a holy man here. We are just mourning the death of my brother. He drowned in the Mediterranean four days ago. You must understand what a tragedy this is for us. We wish to be alone now. Please leave and let us be. *Tizku L'Mitzvot.*" *May you merit good deeds.*

The strangers at the first row dropped their eyes, disappointed.

They don't seem to get it! Ram stewed inside. For a second he thought he would have to ask again, to beg. Then, one by one, they slowly, reluctantly, filed out, saying *Hamakom Yenachem* on their way out. The second and third row followed, and then everyone behind them, until the house resembled a home again, more or less. Only a few close friends and family stayed behind, not to leave the mourners completely on their own.

When Ram turned back to face his father, his heart sank. Chaim just sat there, quiet, his shoulders slumped, his head low. At the same time, Millie arrived from the back of the house and took her place on the sofa.

Ram sat down next to his father. He was tired. All at once his energy dwindled to none.

"Abba, why aren't you discouraging this?"

Chaim didn't reply. He had the prayer book in his hands. He held it tight, his knuckles white. Ram put his hand on them. They were cold and hard. He leaned toward his dad, trying to catch his attention. "Abba?"

"I saw Nir. I really *saw* him," Chaim finally said, his eyes fixed at space beyond his hands. "I was right with him, he showed me things... places."

"I believe you Abba," Millie said. She reached closer to Chaim and gently put her arm around his shoulder. For a brief moment Ram saw how much older she became. She looked like a mother consoling her child. She then looked at Ram, and mouthed without voice, *Please, not now.*

They sat quietly, not uttering a word, each with their thoughts.

Once the chaos subsided, Asher Shalom joined them.

"There is a group of people downstairs," he said. "They won't go away. They are waiting for the *Mekubal* to come. They want to see him and get his blessing."

Ram rolled his eyes, not believing this was still going on.

"Their leader, a nice guy, says his name is Meir Ben-Israel. He wants to come in and talk with you." The last part Asher Shalom addressed to Chaim.

"Call him up," Chaim said without hesitation.

"Wait," Ram jumped from his seat. "He is crazy like all his friends downstairs!" He was convinced this was a scam, a religious fanatic collecting money for some cause, pocketing most of it into his own bank account. Turning to face his father, he said, "Why do you want to speak with him? Don't let him in, Abba."

"Call him up," Chaim repeated, ignoring Ram.

"You know how these parasites can be. If you play their games, they will never leave you alone. All they want is to *schnor...*"

"Call him up!" Chaim's voice was stronger, decisive.

"Okay, okay, no need to get upset." Asher Shalom was happy to comply. "I am going to call him."

Ben-Israel was exactly as Ram imagined him—late twenties or early thirties, average height and skinny build, his beard grown unruly, long uncombed sidelocks dangling from both side of his head. He wore a knitted white *kippah* that covered his entire scalp and wide loose cotton clothes, decorated with vertical blue and white stripes. To complete the look, Ben-Israel was draped with an extra-large *tzitzit* over his shirt, the tassels swung loosely all around him, some of them so long they reached the floor.

Which crazy house did he run from? Ram thought. *No, he didn't have to escape one. He probably lives in one with all his friends, on a rocky hill somewhere in the West Bank.*

As he stepped through the door, Ben-Israel kissed the *mezuzah* on the door frame with utter devotion, raising his eyes to the ceiling as he kissed the hand that just touched the long plastic tube. He then approached Chaim, Ram, and Millie.

"Thank you for seeing me, Reb Levi," he said, bowing slightly, averting Chaim's eyes, looking at his toes instead.

"Sit, sit," Chaim said, pointing to a nearby chair.

"With your permission." Ben-Israel took the chair. He still didn't look at Chaim.

"Bring us some coffee, Chava, and those cookies with the sugar on top," Chaim called to the direction of the kitchen. Then, addressing Ben-Israel, he finally asked, "So tell me, who is this *Mekubal* you are looking for?"

"We have heard rumors he already visited here," Ben-Israel said.

Chaim shot a look at Ram. *You see?* was written all over his face.

"Yes!" Chaim exclaimed. "What is his name? Where does he come from?" he asked, not waiting for the answers to come.

Instead of replying, Ben-Israel said, "I am very sorry for your loss, Reb Levi. Your son, Nir *Zichrono Livracha*, must have been a very special person."

"He was, he was," Chaim nodded. He deflated slightly, shrinking in his spot on the sofa like the air just came out of him.

"No one knows the *Mekubal's* name. We don't know where he lives or where he comes—"

"Is there anything you know about him?" Chaim cut him off, back at the edge of the seat.

"We know quite a lot." By now Ben-Israel looked directly at Chaim's eyes. They were kind and warm. "He appears at *shiva* houses when the crowds are big, and he doesn't stay too long. He mixes in the crowd, not revealing who he is nor the reason for his appearance. He then approaches one of the mourners, blesses them somehow, and leaves. Sometimes he returns to the same *shiva* house more than once, but it's quite rare."

"Do you know what he looks like?" Chaim asked, eager to compare this *Mekubal*'s description with the one he remembered from the previous night.

"That's where it becomes confusing," Ben-Israel admitted. "That's why it's so hard for us to track him down. We heard many stories and reports about him. Some people claim he is a middle-aged Ashkenazi rabbi, others swear he is Yemenite. I have heard one person claiming it's not a man but a woman! Can you believe that?" Ben-Israel snorted.

Chaim's demeanor changed. He didn't seem as excited as before. "I see."

"You probably think it's not the man you saw. Let me be the judge of that. Can you tell me how he looked?"

"How do you know he even saw anyone?" Ram said.

Until that minute Ben-Israel ignored Ram. He slowly turned to face him, nodding. "Fair enough. We have heard rumors; that your father has seen your brother, that he took him places and showed him things."

Rumors. That's why these people are here, because of rumors! Rumors spread faster than the speed it took them to stretch their hands and beg for money. That's why I can't stand this city, these people.

"I see," Chaim said again.

"That's what other mourners told us before. That's why we call him *Mechaye Hametim*. The Resurrector." Ben-Israel paused, waiting for a reaction. He pulled on the tassels of his *tzitzit*, twisting them around his fingers.

When no one talked, he continued. "Do you remember what he looked like? It will be important for us to know, as sometimes, especially after a first sighting, he appears in the same form for a period of time."

Chaim thought for a long time.

"I'm not sure…" he finally said. "It was so crowded here. Lots of people arrived for the service…"

"Abba—"

"No, no, Ram, wait, I do remember. It was brief, but I remember his face, his eyes… but he didn't look like anyone you mentioned!"

"Please, Reb Levi. Just tell me what you remember."

"Okay," Chaim said. "It was a man, for sure. He was not old. His hair and beard were trimmed… very short. He wore simple clothes… maybe a white shirt and jeans? But his eyes… His eyes were deep brown, and they felt," Chaim searched for a word, "…wet."

"Yes," Ben-Israel nodded. "The consistency of the inconsistent. It's just like with the others, seeing someone who does not match most of the previous sightings."

"So how do you explain it?" Chaim asked, baffled.

"We have a theory. We believe that it is Eliyahu Hanavi, and he appears to us in different ways."

Ram gasped. He then laughed an uncontrolled chuckle somewhere between a snort and a schoolgirl's giggle. He rubbed his eyes with his hands, shaking his head in disbelief. Chaim did not share his reaction. He rather focused intently on Ben-Israel.

"So what are you telling me?" Ram asked. "This… this *Mekubal* of yours is actually no other than Elijah the Prophet?

That he is some shape shifter who can change his body to resemble someone else?"

"Yes, it's our theory," Ben-Israel repeated, unapologetically.

"Of course!" Chaim exclaimed. "It makes so much sense! Who else other than Eliyahu Hanavi can bring someone from the dead? Or appears in different shapes? It's just like in those stories—people have real miracles happen to them by a stranger… and it's *never* the same description of the stranger…!"

Ben-Israel nodded, his eyes shining, a smile filling his entire face. He raised his arms in the air, the tassels of his *tzitzit* sprung around him, and he picked up his *kippah* with both hands and put it back on, adjusting it around his head.

Ram was speechless. It amazed him that his father, the rational and logical Chaim Levi, would contemplate such a theory. Yes, his father was religious from birth and always led a God fearing and a God believing life, but this is so irrational. And what is *this*, exactly? Messianism? Voodoo might fit the bill better.

Ram looked around. The small group of people around them, smart people—he knew them his entire life—looked at Ben-Israel with awe. It made him sick to his stomach. Then he caught Tammy's eyes. She looked at him, connected with him, commanded him to calm down, to just let his father go through whatever it is he was going through.

Her eyes said, *Observe it from the sideline and keep an eye on him.*

He smiled at her. At least he was not alone.

CHAPTER 10

CHAIM

A sharp smell greets me: disinfectant and industrial cleaners. The lights are bright. Large signs in blue and white direct visitors to different departments: Emergency Room. Intensive Care Unit. Pediatric ICU. Cardiology. Imaging. Maternity. Neurology. Orthopedics. Oncology.

I don't need to read the signs. I know where I am and where I need to go. I have been through these halls countless times. My feet take me where I need to go. They remember what I want to forget. They take me past the main reception area, the donor recognition plaques on the wall, the cafeteria and gift shop. They take me past the elevator and to the staircase marked A, up the stairs two floors. Then they turn me to the left and down a maze of halls. I pass more reception desks, waiting rooms, nurse stations. They lead me around empty hospital rooms and abandoned hospital beds lining the corridors. Gurneys, some carts with cleaning equipment, others with food trays and medicine. Wheelchairs. IV lines dangling from poles on wheels. Oxygen balloons.

The room is at the end of a corridor. I don't look at the sign above me; I know what it says. Oncology. Stopping now is not an option. I slowly go down the hall. The smell is sharper, obtrusive. The smell that comes just before death. The rooms along this hallway are dark and empty. Light comes from the room at the end, and I can hear people talking, laughing.

I stop. I must take a long breath. I know who is inside. What I don't know is if I am ready to face them.

The room has gray linoleum floor and pale-green walls. Fluorescent lights flood it from overhead fixtures, painting everything in a sick whitewash. Medical instruments, whose names or purpose I have never known, litter the space—on metal carts, poles, some even suspended from the ceiling.

It is a private room. Most patients didn't have the luxury to have a room for themselves. I was able to arrange it with some connections.

In the middle of the room stands a large hospital bed, cream colored and adjustable. A single chair stands by the bed. The blinds in the windows shut closed, blocking outside light.

On the bed, just like in the last two months of her life, lays my wife, my dear wife, Sarah. She is propped up, a blue cotton snood covering her head. Underneath it, her head is round and bald. How I cried when she started losing her hair. But Sarah, she was the strong one. Always the strong one.

Her face is puffed up, and she is weak, so weak, but the eyes are the same kind green eyes, the smile is the same welcoming smile, the one promising—*life is good!*

She wears her housecoat and some makeup, not too much, just the right amount that makes her glow. Her nails are done and painted in the same shade of red she always loved, the color of the anemones that grew wildly on the hills behind her childhood home, she used to say.

Nir is in the room with her. He sits at the edge of the bed, one ankle relaxed on the opposite knee. He holds her hands in his. They are laughing at something. They are happy.

I freeze in both awe and dismay. I can't go any further. Right in front of me are the two loves I have lost, in this room that I came to hate, that took my wife away.

I stay in the same spot. Sarah and Nir don't notice me standing there. They are immersed in a lively discussion. Nir talks, and his mother listens intently, nodding or shaking her head here and there, exclaiming in surprise or asking a question. I can't hear what Nir tells her. I can only read their body language. The machines all around us are beeping and gurgling, sucking and puffing. The noises don't bother Sarah and Nir, but they shield their conversation from me.

It is just like when Nir was younger, and Sarah was still alive. Every time that Nir needed a helping hand or a listening ear, he would go to Sarah. She would embrace and comfort him. She listened to every story, solved every problem.

One night, when Nir was not *bar mitzvah* yet, Sarah told me about a girl Nir liked.

"It's adorable," she said.

"Adorable? He is just a little boy!" I started fuming. "Where did he even meet her?"

"At Bnei Akiva. They are in the same group. You know, they were preparing for *Shabbat Irgun*. He is drawing and painting the artwork on their walls, and I think she is one of the other talented kids."

I dismissed it. He was still a boy. He should not have been in the coed youth group. That's what would happen when you mix boys and girls. Their adolescent hormones were out of control. It's not healthy. In any case, he was wasting too much time over there.

But not Sarah. She was smitten by the fact that he liked that girl. She wanted to know who the girl was, where she lived, who her parents were, which synagogue they were members of.

"You are like an adolescent girl yourself," I partially teased, partially scolded her. "He is too young, and he will not start running now after some girl, and that's that!" It was my final word on the matter.

The next day I told Nir he must forget about that girl, any girl. Nir didn't protest. He just mumbled what I believed was consent to my command. His reaction didn't reveal whether he was upset with my decision. What I didn't know back then was that he secretly, behind my back, consulted with Sarah. And my wife, God bless her soul, encouraged him, suggested ways he could meet that girl without my knowledge.

She brought it up as a joke some years later, during the time her cancer came back. It had metastasized into other parts of her body, and she needed a complicated surgery to try to remove an area around her spine. If the surgery would be successful, her doctor said, she had a good chance of beating it. But the prognosis was not good.

Before she went into surgery, Sarah wanted us to celebrate life. We decorated the house for a party and invited some of our dearest friends and family. Millie baked Sarah's favorite walnut crescent cookies, and everyone lent a hand making her beloved dishes. Sarah insisted it would not be a sad day or anxious time, but rather a happy day, celebrating life to its fullest.

For the party, she prepared a surprise for all of us—an album with pictures and some stories she wrote about each one of us. She said this is how she wanted to remember us before she went into surgery. Everyone prayed for her fast recovery, many of us avoiding the unavoidable possibility— that she might die. She was so strong, my beautiful Sarah.

On the page she dedicated for Nir, she wrote a poem. She loved rhyming, and though she admitted not being much good at it, she didn't care how it sounded. It made her feel happy and warm and sometimes giggly, she used to say. The poem went something like this:

Nir—my sandwich one
Peanut butter and jelly
He won't be bullied
Or punched in the belly
Stubborn and strong minded
Just like his daddy
My little Don Juan
Breaking girls' hearts—did I mention Rachelly?

Next to the poem, which she handwritten in her rounded script, she affixed a picture of Nir standing next to a girl. They were about the same height, wearing their Bnei Akiva uniforms—Nir in khaki pants and a white shirt, the girl, Rachelly, in an ankle length dark skirt and white blouse. They both had the blue youth group tie around their neck, rolled and pinned in the front with the organization's emblem. The photo was taken at night, and the flashlight made their faces flat and ghostlike. Both were smiling to the camera, a semi-shy, semi-secretive look on their face.

"You were so sweet here," Sarah said when we all looked at the album together, pointing to Nir's picture. "Her name was Rachelly, right? Or did I mess that up? With this cancer in me, you can never know!"

"Imma, your cancer is below your neckline, nowhere near your brain," Nir goofed back at her, laughing. They had this easiness I never had when talking about her disease, about any life struggle. It was their way to deal with the situation, a way I couldn't share, but I was patient enough to allow them to use it.

"So who is this girl, anyway?" I asked, diverting the discussion back to safer territories.

"She was Nir's sweetheart in Bnei Akiva. He was in *Shevet Ma'alot*. They were the artists of their tribe, and they both painted their entire room. What happened to her, Nir? Where is she these days?"

Nir didn't reply. He blushed a bit, looking at his mother in an all-knowing way. I think she then caught herself and the mistake she made. She started laughing, a hearty laugh, her eyes tearing up. Everyone else started laughing with her, her laugh contagious. She made them all feel at ease.

"What is so funny?" I didn't get it.

"I…. I just… realized…." she tried to say, but between laughing hysterically, crying, and hiccupping, I had to wait for her to calm down first. "I just realized that you don't even know about her!" she finally said, "I told you about her. I remember now. You were so upset, forbidding him from being in touch with her. It was ridiculous."

I felt my face redden and my ears heat up. "What are you talking about? That was the end of it," I looked at Nir, demanding, "Wasn't it?"

"Leave him alone. It was not his fault," Sarah said. "I actually encouraged him. I made sure you wouldn't know anything. After all, how hard was that? You had no idea…"

How could I have been mad at her? Now, with cancer inside of her, the night before an operation to save her life?

"You tricked me, and I don't appreciate it," I said. Then, smiling, I asked Nir, "So, did you ask her to be your girlfriend?"

We looked at each other. The ice was broken, and we both started laughing, joined by Sarah and everyone else.

Since Sarah passed away, I tried talking to him, connecting with him the way Sarah did. It didn't work. We never had that connection before, and creating it now was too hard for both of us. We gave up early. And it just got worse.

Looking at them now, sitting together on her hospital bed, I am envious—of her, for being so easygoing and understanding, for her ability to relate so effortlessly. Of him, for that special connection he had with his mom. But they are both dead now, dead and gone. Are they really? My heart aches; a phantom hand squeezes it, yielding a few more drops of anguish.

As I stand there, observing my dear Sarah and Nir, the room's noises slowly cease, and they are replaced with music. At first, the change is unnoticeable. Then the music becomes clearer, louder. An acoustic guitar is playing, and a raspy voice sings a familiar tune. A Carlebach song, one I have heard many times before. Sarah loved Rabbi Carlebach and his melodies. When she listened to him, her eyes brightened, their outer corners lifted slightly. She would close her eyes, her face smooth and relaxed, her head bobbing gently to the tune. You could actually *see* her spirit lifting.

In her hospital bag, the one I hated so much and was the first thing I threw away after cancer beat her, she packed a couple of his compact discs and a CD player. In this very room, the nurses played them for her so many times. It helped ease the pain. She hated painkillers; they made her feel drowsy and sleep for hours, and she wanted to stay awake, to feel alive, pain and all. Her remedy of choice was Carlebach, the *singing rabbi*.

The music grows louder. It comes from all around us and vibrates inside me. My heart is pounding, my teeth are rattling.

Sarah and Nir continue ignoring me and the music. They keep talking, unaware of their surroundings.

I finally unfreeze and start moving, walking slowly toward them. My movements are slow and sluggish, like walking against a stream in a sudden desert flash flood. Each leg weighs a ton, and my arms push through the air, slicing and thrusting. The toy airplane in my hand slows me down, but I won't let go of it. When I finally reach the bed, I am panting. I need to rest. I lean both hands on the foot of the bed and slump my head on them, breathing hard. I stand like that for some time until I catch my breath, and then I look up.

Nir and Sarah are quiet. Both are looking at me.

The music stops abruptly. My ears ring, as they are not used to the quiet. Nir and Sarah don't seem to notice. They just look at me.

Then Sarah turns to Nir.

"Please take care of Abba for me, Niri. Promise me you will. He is such a proud man, just like you, and he will never admit his feelings."

Nir listens to her, but his gaze is still on me.

"I don't have much time, my sweetheart," she continues. "Ram has started his life now in the army, and Millie is so young… I need to know someone will be there for Abba. Will you?" Is she begging?

"And what about me? Who will take care of me when you are gone?" His eyes are still on me.

"Niri, Niri, I will be there with you all the time." She leans closer to him, her hand weak and veiny, reaching him at his bicep. He turns his head slowly, deliberately, to look at her. "When you can't feel me, listen to Reb Carlebach. My spirit is in his songs."

Nir lowers his eyes. I don't know if he made a promise or not. He doesn't say a thing. Instead, he stands and turns around to face his mother. He leans down to kiss her, a kiss on each side of her face. They are goodbye kisses, long, sad kisses. He then turns again, this time to the entrance, and runs out of the room.

Sarah is still here, and I don't want to leave her. Deep down I know that I must follow Nir, but here is my wife, my beloved *Beshert*, whom I haven't seen for five years since the hated cancer took her away from me.

I sit on the bed where Nir sat before. I stretch my hand out. "Sarah," I say.

She looks at me. Or she looks through me. I'm not sure which one it is.

"Sarah, it is me, Chaim. Can you hear me? Can you say something?"

She blinks as if a recognition switch turned on inside of her. She starts humming, and then her lips move, and she is singing the Carlebach tune.

She doesn't see me. She is not going to talk to me. I realize that. It is just like the boys at the dorms.

I get up and leave the room, not looking back.

CHAPTER 11

Tuesday, Third Day of the Shiva

RAM

"Can you tell me who else have seen him?" Chaim was eager to know.

"Yes," Ben-Israel replied. "But first I want to do a *Farbrengen*." When he saw the question on Chaim's face, he added, "A Chassidic spiritual gathering. May I call my friends to join us?"

Ram was alarmed. That's the last thing he wanted, to bring more riffraff like Ben-Israel into their house. He started objecting when his father said, "Yes, of course, call them up."

Ram couldn't hide his dismay. "Abba, this is not the place for a Chassidic gathering! We are sitting *shiva*, for God's sake, not celebrating a memorial for a dead rabbi!"

"Ram, come with me for a moment," his father commanded. He stood and waited for Ram to follow. Ben-Israel jumped to his feet at the same time.

"Reb Levi, I understand if it's not the best time. My apologies for imposing…"

"Sit down, Ben-Israel," Chaim said, "and call your friends to come up here. And you," he looked at Ram, "move!"

He led Ram to the master bedroom and closed the door behind them. The blanket and pillow were rolled together in a heap on the bed, the dirty laundry hamper overflowing.

Piles of newspapers covered the chest, sleeping pills and painkiller tablets on the nightstand. The room smelled stale.

"Listen to me, Ram," Chaim started. "This is the first time in my life that I feel a positive connection with Nir."

Ram sneered, "Too bad he is dead!"

"He is not dead to me. Not yet."

"Abba, you are going crazy!" Ram shouted. He was furious and frustrated. His father was losing his mind right in front of him. "Look around you! Where is Nir? You saw him yourself dead, drowned! For two freaking years you didn't want to talk to him. You said he was dead to you. We tried everything to make you see him and talk with him… Now that he is dead you don't accept that either?"

"I made many mistakes, Ram," Chaim dropped his eyes, looking at his fingernails. "These years without your Imma were not easy for me. You were not here to see how Nir and I fought all the time… And then, this business with the woman…" he trailed off.

"This business, as you call it, almost killed Nir, and if you were a bit less egocentric, thinking a bit less about yourself and about what people would say about you, you would have seen how much he needed you!"

Chaim turned away.

It's always the same thing, Ram thought. *He just can't face the truth.*

"I am dealing with that now, Ram," Chaim whispered. "Please let me do it my way. I have seen Nir… and I want to see him again, at least to tell him enough so that he forgives me."

"Do you really believe you see him? It's an illusion; a fantasy!"

Chaim shook his head violently. With his right hand, he rubbed the front pocket of his pants.

"How do you see him?" Ram pushed, harder than he would ever allow himself with his dad. "Tell me, how exactly do you see him?"

Chaim looked at him. "The man, just before I fainted, gave me something of Nir." He quickly averted his eyes. "You won't believe it, anyway."

"How do you expect me to believe in this... this nonsense?"

"I don't know." Chaim now looked directly at Ram. "All I know is that it keeps happening. And there must be a reason for it. We are believers, and God works in mysterious ways."

"I don't like that Ben-Israel guy. And his theory... It sounds like a cult."

"I know, but I must try if I want to understand it. I have seen him..."

Ram paused to look at his father's eyes. "Okay," he finally said, defeated. "If you must. But please promise me to be careful, Abba. I don't have a good feeling about Ben-Israel. If his intentions are not after your money—"

"My money?" Chaim scoffed.

"Yes, your money, Abba. If it's not the money, he has some other motive. I just don't know what it is."

With that, they returned to the living room. "Where are your friends?" Chaim asked Ben-Israel. "Are they too shy?"

Ben-Israel smiled. "Just waiting for my signal that everything is okay." He picked up his cell phone and punched in a number. When his friend answered, he said one word, "*Ta'alu.*" Come up.

A few minutes later the door opened, and a slow stream of people filed in. Some of them were in the house before, during the evening service. Ram expected some commonality amongst them, assuming all of them were weirdos like Ben-Israel. He imagined them living in tents and shacks on the rocky hills of Samaria in an illegal settlement, clothes unkempt, using a natural water spring in the middle of nowhere for their personal grooming, food provided by free ranging chickens and goats. What he saw surprised him. They were not a homogenous group. Most did not fit their leader's first impression.

A couple of them did fit the bill—they wore baggy cotton pants and shirts, sported long dreadlocks of hair, wrapped around and hanging in big clumps behind their backs. The rest of the group included *yeshiva* looking men—in black suits, white shirts, matching dark neckties, and black fedora hats, which gave them their nickname *black hatters*—several modern orthodox guys of various ages, and three men who did not look religious at all. Ram could tell by their *kippahs*, made out of shiny crumpled cloth that didn't fit their head shapes but rather awkwardly sat on their scalps like erupted volcanoes. One of the men used a newspaper to cover his head in place of a *kippah*. Someone pointed out for him the box of *yamakas*, tucked next to the stack of prayer books. He picked one up and replaced the makeshift head cover.

Ben-Israel introduced the little group to Chaim, Ram, and Millie. They sat down on folding chairs in a semicircle, the mourners' sofa their focal point.

Ben-Israel took the lead. "My brothers, this is a special evening for all of us. Our *Mekubal*, the one we believe is Eliyahu Hanavi, appeared again. This time to this *tzadik*," he pointed at Chaim, while his friends nodded their agreement. "This *tzadik*—a righteous man!—who sits *shiva* for his son, Nir Ben Chaim." He omitted *zichrono livracha*. Blessed be his memory.

"Nir passed away four days ago. How did he die, Reb Levi?" he asked Chaim.

"He drowned in the Mediterranean."

Heads shook around the room. Some men uttered quiet words, spread their arms to their sides, looked to the ceiling with pleading eyes, then brought their hands together, kissing the tips of their fingers.

"Drowned at sea. What a horrible way to go," Ben-Israel shook his head from side to side too. "You have been blessed, Reb Levi. The *Tzadik* Eliyahu has chosen to visit you and given you the ability to see your son!"

"Yes!" One of the dreadlocks voiced from the circle.

"Let us drink to that and rejoice in the opportunity you have been given!"

Ram observed the black-hatter sitting next to him taking a vodka bottle from his backpack and a stack of disposable plastic shot glasses. *Of course, these men are always prepared. Weddings, funerals—they always have a hard drink handy.* The bottle moved around the room, and no one skipped the chance to drink.

"*L'chaim!*" Ben-Israel declared. To life! "To Chaim Ben..." He looked at Chaim, his brows raised in unison with his hand holding the little cup.

"Ben Yosef HaLevi," Chaim completed for him. Son of Yosef the Levite.

"To Chaim Ben Yosef HaLevi and to Nir Ben Chaim HaLevi!" Everyone brought their plastic shots up and exclaimed, "*L'chaim.*" They drained the clear liquid.

Ben-Israel started humming a tune. Ram strained his ears to hear it. Ben-Israel closed his eyes as he hummed, then chanted, louder as the song progressed, his hands clapping his knees, emphasizing passages in the music.

A Carlebach tune.

Ben-Israel's friends joined in, following his cue. Ram looked around. *Drinking and singing in a* shiva *house! What next? Dancing the* mitzvah *dance?*

Chaim ignored the other guests bewildered looks. He too joined Ben-Israel and his circle of friends. The tune repeated, the group singing it again and again, each time with stronger voices. Two of them stood on their feet and rocked their bodies, their eyes closed, their entire body animated with their spiritual experience.

The room closed in on Ram. Sweat covered the nape of his neck. The heat was unbearable. Newcomers came through the door. They stood around the room, watching the strange group quietly, the singing, his father chanting.

Ram couldn't tell how long this took. He did not join in. When he tried to catch his father's attention, Chaim waved him with the back of his hand and continued singing along. Eventually, Ben-Israel stopped singing and opened his eyes. The men beside him followed his lead until all voices died. As one, they swayed lightly in their seats like stalks of wheat in a small field. They looked at Ben-Israel, their eyes shining, waiting patiently for his words.

Ben-Israel stood. Looking at Chaim, he started, "There are many sightings of the *Tzadik* Eliyahu Hanavi. We only know about a small portion of them, maybe one for every five visits. The common thread is the mourners, sitting for loved ones, the majority passed away unexpectedly before their time. Shimon here," he nodded at one of the *yeshiva* black hatters, "can swear he met witnesses of sightings at a Muslim mourners' tent in Jaffa. Many of us don't believe it's the real thing but a copycat. Why would Eliyahu go to non-Jews and give them this gift?"

Shimon had an apologetic expression on his face. He shrugged and raised his hands in a "don't blame the messenger" gesture.

"We know of a famous singer, I won't mention any names, whose wife died. They had problems in their marriage. He told me that she wanted to send the kids to religious schools, while he forbade it." Ben-Israel paused for effect. "Eliyahu Hanavi came to him, and he was able to see how wrong he was. Immediately after the *shiva* had ended, he took his two boys out of the secular school and sent them to a religious one. He has since done *teshuva*, living a complete religious life…"

Several observers in the room whispered to each other, trying to guess who the celebrity was, as there were many likely candidates.

"Tell him about the mayor!" someone shouted.

"Yes, that was incredible!" another added.

"Right, the mayor," Ben-Israel agreed. "You notice I don't mention any names, as most of the people prefer to stay anonymous. They don't want people to think they are crazy—"

Ram snorted audibly. Ben-Israel did not pay attention. Or he was ignoring Ram, like someone well accustomed to skeptics.

"So they prefer to keep it quiet. This is why we don't know about most of the incidents where Mechaye Hametim appeared." He turned around, looking toward the kitchen and the women who stood there listening intently. "May I have some water? It will be a great *mitzvah* if you can get me a glass." One of his friends jumped off his chair and ran to the kitchen. He reappeared quickly, a tall glass of water in hand.

"Thank you, Gilad." He blessed on the water and drank a few sips. "So, the mayor," he continued. "I won't say which city, of course, nor who died in his case."

As if he really cares about confidentiality, Ram thought. *I must give it to him, he is a careful son of a bitch.*

"When the mayor was sitting *shiva* with his family, it was a very private affair. They sat one day in his villa, letting the press and other politicians who came to console him, but then he moved to another house, one of his siblings' place. Naturally they didn't announce it so they could have privacy. Only their closest friends and family were privy to the new location. His chief of staff managed that list very closely. He was in the house when it happened, and he later told me about it in person."

The room was soundless, everyone's attention on Ben-Israel as he told the story.

"One evening, when they prepared to pray *Mincha* and *Ma'ariv*, they didn't have a *minyan*, only nine men. They did what anyone would do—someone went outside to scout for a tenth person. I spoke with that guy personally. He told me the streets were deserted, very surreal, as if everyone had left the city. After walking for a few minutes around the block, he came across a beggar. An old man, short and scruffy looking, sitting on a bench at the edge of a small parkette. He approached the old beggar, even though he could not tell whether the man was Jewish or not. He tried to find signs—a kippah on his head, a light skin color, or a Hebrew newspaper in his belonging—but in the diminishing daylight he found no telling signs.

"He asked the old man if he would come to complete a *minyan* in a mourners' house. The beggar agreed. That was good enough. They walked together to the house. The most peculiar thing that he noticed about the beggar was that he didn't smell like a homeless person, but at the time, he was just thankful for that. The beggar was shy and quietly said, 'Amen,' after every blessing. Someone offered him a prayer book, but he refused. At the end of the service, the mayor thanked him for coming and invited him to eat something. The beggar declined. Turning to leave, he stopped in his tracks, faced the mayor again, reached closer to him, and hugged him."

"What happened? Did he see the person who died?" Chaim asked. His excitement was clear.

"Yes!" Ben-Israel replied. "That is the common thread amongst all these occurrences. The mayor was very ill afterward, unconscious, hanging between life and death. It never leaked to the media. His staff and family did a great job keeping it away from those vultures, claiming some family emergency, which was not far from the truth. When he came through, he conferred with his chief of staff and told him what happened, what he saw."

"What did he see?" Chaim asked. He was sitting at the edge of the sofa.

"How come you know all of this?" Ram asked, not trying to hide the sarcasm in his voice. "And your circle of friends here?"

"Great questions!" Ben-Israel exclaimed. "I don't know all the details of what he saw, so I don't know all of *this*, as you put it. We have been following Mechaye Hametim for eight years now, and people are talking. They believe in the same things we believe, and they are sharing their stories. And to answer your question, Reb Chaim, the mayor has seen many miracles while he was unconscious. He saw the past, the present, and the future. He closed open wounds with the person he lost and was able to come out alive."

Ben-Israel's gang relaxed in their chairs, smiling when hearing what they perceived to be the story's climax.

"So," Ram said, "did you ever see him, in person?"

"You are ever the skeptic, aren't you? All right, be like that. Yes, I believe I have seen him. I didn't realize it until several years later."

Chaim gasped. "Who did you lose?" he asked.

"No one in my family," Ben-Israel replied. "My parents are healthy and strong, *Baruch HaShem*." Thank God. "My siblings are living all around the world, but all are well. And I have not yet married and fathered a child."

"So how did you see him?" Ram challenged him.

"My closest friend died in a car crash. We went to Ben Gurion University. Tzvi was in medical school, and I was doing my MBA."

He has a university education? Ram didn't expect this tidbit of information. *Ben-Israel, the leader of these nomads, the one who looked like a nomad himself, studying business management at university? What's next? Will he announce that he is running for office?*

"During our third year, he borrowed my car one night and drove north to Yavne. He was tutoring there. He lost control of the car, no one knows why, and drove into the incoming traffic. He crashed head-on into a semitrailer. Killed instantly."

"But you were not sitting *shiva* for him." Ram tried to find holes in Ben-Israel theories.

"That's true, and the *Mekubal* didn't come for me. I wasn't the one who needed to see Tzvi after his death. It was his mother. I saw when the *Mekubal* came over and shook her hand. It was the strangest thing. The *Mekubal* was an old rabbi, ultra-orthodox looking, one who wouldn't touch any woman. And here he was, looking at her and shaking her hand.

"She fell ill shortly after, and when she got better, I heard she had some visions of Tzvi. I dismissed it then as a fantasy of a grieving mother. Several years later I started hearing similar stories—*shiva* house, someone coming, touching one of the grieving families, who then starts seeing their loved ones. It was just like what happened with Tzvi's mom."

"Ben-Israel." Ram had had enough. He wanted them all out of the house. "This is all nice and fascinating. But my father, my sister, and I—we are exhausted. I must ask you and your friends to leave us now. If my father sees anyone that looks slightly like your Messiah, we will let you know. Okay?"

Ben-Israel looked surprised, but to his credit, he stayed silent. He looked at Chaim for directions. Chaim merely nodded. Ram had never seen him looking so small and defeated. Ben-Israel got the hint. He stood up to leave, followed by his friends.

"Please, if you see anything, anyone, give me a call at this number," Ben-Israel said and gave Chaim a small card. "It's confidential. Your story, or any of your personal details, will not leak out. I give you my word."

"Don't you think it is a bit too late for that?" Ram said. "Where did the mob earlier today come from if someone didn't spread a rumor already?" He looked accusingly at Ben-Israel and his group.

"If you think it was us, think twice," Ben-Israel said. "We have waited outside, and we have heard the rumors like everybody else. We were not the ones to spread them."

He then picked up the glass of water, handed it to Chava at the kitchen's door, and walked to the apartment's entrance. Just before he stepped through the door, he turned back to face Chaim, Ram, and Millie, and said, "*Hamakom yenachem etchem betoch shea'r aveley tzion ve'Yerushalaim.*"

His friends followed his lead, each uttering, "*Hamakom yenachem.*"

CHAPTER 12

CHAIM

I exit the hospital room. My face is wet. I hadn't been aware that I was crying. I wipe my eyes with my sleeve. I retrace my steps back to the main entrance and avoid looking around, focusing only on one goal: to leave this place.

I reach the main lobby. Bright light floods it, coming from outside through the glass front panels. Its surprising ferocity temporarily blinds me. Is it high noon already? Time had passed quicker than I thought. Another thought occurs to me. There is no *time* in this place. Only the sites Nir wants me to see, and the distance between them. I prepare myself to expect nothing once I step out of the hospital.

I walk slowly toward the entrance, shielding my eyes with the hand that holds the little stone. As I near the doors, they slide slowly to either side, widening a gap between them. Through the opening, the light breaks in with all its might. My eyes close reflexively, a dark rectangle in the middle of my shuttered vision.

I stand this way for some time, waiting for my vision to return, for the phantom shapes to dissipate. When I finally open my eyes, I raise both hands in front of them. I am still holding onto Nir's airplane. I use it to block some of the light in front of me, the uneven shape of the wings large enough for this purpose.

I step outside. I squint my eyes against the light. I don't know if I am still in the parking lot, the one I came through into the hospital, or whether I have been transported some-where else.

I must keep moving. I hope the glaring light will change if I move somewhere else.

I look down in front of me, still shielding my eyes with my hands and the model airplane, and I take one step at a time. The ground is gray and nondescript. I don't see any marks. I keep going, faster and more determined. My arms ache after holding them up to my eyes far too long. I need to find a better way to filter the light. I take the knitted *kippah* off my head and hold it flat against my eyes. I can see through the tiny holes between each small knit.

I continue this way for some time, switching hands as the one holding the *kippah* grows tired. The air around me feels more comfortable, not as freezing as before. The light, on the other hand, seems to grow brighter.

Red. My vision through the little holes between my *kippah's* threads registers the dark red before my feet feel through the soles of my shoes—something sticky. It's on the ground. I stop in my tracks and lean down, carefully extending my hand to the floor. I touch it with my fingertip and look closely at the red substance. Blood.

Where am I? I panic. All I wanted was to see Nir again. To save him this time. But what happened here? Was I even close to him? I can't tell.

Suddenly, the bright light dims around me, leaving me in the dark. My eyes must adjust again. It feels like being in a petri dish under an enormous microscope and someone has adjusted the light from the widest setting and focused it on the narrowest position. One intense beam remains, its light illuminates a circle on the ground. In the middle of the circle—

No, no, that can't be!

Just like the pictures and news clips. But why?
Nir, what is it that you want of me?
—a bus lies upside down.

The bus is lying on its roof, which is mostly smashed inward as if a mighty giant punched it in. Deep scratches line the sides of the bus while the windows are completely shattered, their frames misshapen. One of the front wheels is spinning. Smoke rises from the engine compartment. The smell reaches me. It stings my eyes and fills my nostrils.

And all around it, bodies of children are thrown on the ground, little bodies torn and mutilated, rivers of blood flowing every which way. They are still and frozen. They are all dead.

I suddenly notice movement inside the bus. Someone cries. It sounds like a woman. I can't see her face. A shape crawls with tremendous difficulty through the wreckage, in the narrow space between the caved-in ceiling and the rows of upside-down chairs. Her hair is matted to her forehead, covering most of her face. She is crying and grunting, snuffling, crying some more. The woman pulls something inside the bus. No, not something, but someone. She is pulling a kid or another small person, I can't say for sure.

A fire erupts at the front end of the bus. I'm afraid the engine will blow at any moment. There are more wails from that area, but no one moves other than the woman. She pulls the person she is trying to help with growing urgency while glancing back at the fire.

I am frozen in place. The numbers pop in my head with the drama of a news announcer on the eve of war. Nine dead. Seven kids, ages seven and eight. One female teacher. Age thirty-nine. Left a husband and three boys. One driver, age fifty-eight. Left a wife, four children, and two grandchildren.

Twenty-five wounded. Three in critical condition. Five lost limbs. The rest suffered less critical injuries. One of them was my Nir.

Eighteen. The number for *chai*, life. He was eighteen. He finished high school several months earlier. Nir always had difficulties at school. Since his mother died, he had an even harder time focusing on his studies. He barely passed his *Bagruyot*, the matriculation exams. He did not seem to care. Once school was over and he returned home from the *yeshiva*, he closed himself in his room for hours on end. He waited for his army enlistment day, which was a few months away.

I begged him to find a job, threatened to take away privileges, screamed that I would throw him out unless he pays rent—nothing seemed to work. We didn't know how to communicate anymore. Maybe we never knew how.

Then things just changed. Instead of arguing all the time, he stayed away from me. He found a night shift job at a restaurant as a busboy. He left the house before I came back from work and returned after I left for the morning service. He didn't last there a month. He then traveled around the country. Neighbors told me they spotted him at the ramp for highway 40, hitchhiking. When I called him, he would vaguely say he was staying with one friend or another.

Ram filled in the details for me later. One of Nir's friends suggested he should replace him on a school trip as an adult chaperone. The friend worked for a company—if you can even call it that—which provided adults and security guards to groups on day trips, mostly elementary schools and nursing homes. The friend had a wedding to attend and could not go that day. Nir would replace him. It was an easy gig—go on the bus with the class and their teacher. Don't speak too much. Count the kids every time they move from one place to another. Accompany the kids on the trip. Decent pay. Nir took it without hesitation. The day passed without a hitch. Ram showed me the last text Nir sent him before the accident:

> With sixty little noisy kids on a bus! But I actually
> am enjoying it :-) Would you believe that?

It happened on the way back. The police investigation was not conclusive. They suspected an animal jumped to the road and scared the bus driver. But there were no witnesses, and the survivors were distracted inside the crowded bus. The driver lost control. The bus burst through the road's security barrier and rolled downhill until it stopped upside down in a ravine, parallel to the highway.

I snap out of my daze and run toward the bus. I look all around me, searching for Nir's face in the bodies scattered around. If he is not here, how would he be saved from the fire in the bus?

I reach one of the windows. The shattered glass crunches under the soles of my shoes. From this position I see more clearly what happened inside the bus. There are more kids, moving, moaning, squeezed together in unnatural positions.

Backpacks, spilled snacks, and water bottles litter every available spot around them. Behind the bus, several children roam around aimlessly. A few kids are sitting on the ground, staring at nowhere in particular. One sucks on his thumb. An adult, a teacher or maybe a parent, helps wounded kids out of the bus. He carries them through a wide hole on that side of the bus and puts them gently on the ground, instructing them to hurry, run away from the burning vehicle.

I see the woman on my side of the ruined vehicle. She is still trying to pull the same person. She grunts with the effort.

I now have a direct vision behind the crooked backseat of one of the hanging chairs. I see who it is. Nir. My heart drops.

He is unconscious and has a small gash on his forehead. His face looks peaceful, but his body hangs upside down. His narrow shoulders support him at the ceiling—now the floor—of the turned bus, and the rest of his body is vertical, held up between the seats with one twisted leg. The other leg is folded and hangs loosely close to his body. I move along the side of the bus and see that one of Nir's feet is stuck under a chair directly above him. His hiking shoe is jammed into a metal bracket supporting the chair. The woman, trying to pull him out of the bus, doesn't see his predicament. The more she pulls, the worse his foot twists and traps him in place.

I root my foot on the window frame to push myself up. Sharp glass cuts into my hands as I use them to leverage myself into the bus. Then I hold the back of the seat to hold myself from falling back. I stretch up to reach for Nir's foot. I try twisting it, but as my hand reaches his shoe and cannot keep its hold, my brain registers that I can't make any changes here! I tried and failed before. I scream in frustration! There isn't sufficient space to clear the foot out, and I don't think the woman will be able to save him. But then she yanks Nir with all her might, and he comes flying into her arms.

She doesn't panic. She crawls in the narrow space around Nir and squeezes her upper body onto the glass covered ground. She calls the man outside for help, waving her hands to catch his attention. When she is sure he saw her, she turns back to Nir and crawls back next to him. The man leans into the bus through the broken window. He grabs Nir under the armpits, trying to keep Nir's head rested on his chest. The woman picks Nir's legs, and she helps the man by raising Nir's bottom and moving him across the window's frame. From that point on, the man carries Nir on his own. He runs with him for safety and lays him on the road. He then runs back to the bus to help the woman out.

She seems exhausted. Instead of saving herself, she is hunched over her arms, breathing heavily. Her hair is clumped in thick wet strands all around her head.

"Quick, crawl out of there!" The man shouts. He bends down and reaches his hands in to help her.

She raises her head up, "There are more kids in here!" she cries. Determined, she pushes herself up on all four and turns around. She shoves a dirty sleeved arm and pushes the wet strands of hair out of her eyes. I finally see her face.

It is her.

CHAPTER 13

Tuesday, Third Day of the Shiva

RAM

Ben-Israel and his friends finally left close to midnight. With them, most of the visitors and curious onlookers filed quietly out of the apartment. The room fell silent. Then voices erupted from everyone. Besides Chaim and Ram, there were Millie, Chava and her husband, Asher Shalom, and a couple of cousins who volunteered to cook meals and clean up the daily mess. Ram didn't see Tammy and couldn't remember her leaving. He was not sure how much of this Ben-Israel business she had witnessed. *If she did, she must think by now that my family is crazy.* The thought was grim. He texted her quickly.

> It's a madhouse. Were you here to see it??? :(
> I need you!

Chaim was excited. He was talking to no one in particular and to all of them at once. "Did you see *that*? Wasn't that *amazing*? I can't believe it. Eliyahu Hanavi in *my* house, touching me, blessing me. And all the people this happened to before!" He was up on his feet now, pacing from one end of the living room to the other.

Asher Shalom, ever the religiously zealous in his practice, said, "We have to go to Rabbi Zechariah with this, ask his opinion! No, he is not important enough... maybe Rabbi

Shapira? He might be the right one for something like this… Or it would be imprudent for us to go to any rabbi. I think this must go to the Rishon Le'tzion! This must go to the Holy of Holies!"

Chava, looking intently at her brother, said, "Do you actually believe you saw Nir? Where did you see him? What did he tell you?"

Millie was silent. She was very quiet during the entire evening, and now she closed up further. She held her siddur, her index finger tucked in to hold the page she was on. Ram guessed she was saying *Tehillim*. She said it vigorously, with the faith only the young and naive can have. The ancient hymns of the Psalms found their way into many wounded souls throughout the generations, giving hope and solace in times of need. She was not much different.

"Am I the only one here who thinks this is crazy?" Ram raised his voice. He mainly tried to catch his father's attention. They all hushed and looked at him. "This is totally crazy," he repeated, searching for words that articulate his frustration. "*Eliyahu Hanavi*? A *Mekubal* who is bringing the dead back from the grave? Where is Nir?" His voice peaked, trembling. "He is dead! Dead… People are not coming from their graves…" He broke down, stood up, and rushed to his room, shutting the door behind him.

Tammy was in his room, sitting on his bed, leafing through an old picture album. When Ram noticed her, she was looking at him, patiently waiting for him to say something. Instead, he dropped beside her and held her, crying. Her touch comforted him. He felt safe and protected. Her warm breath on his neck, her smell, the soft skin—they all reminded him of his Imma. How he wished she would be here now.

When he calmed down, Tammy asked, "Do you want to talk about it?"

He nodded. Talking with Tammy seemed to be the only normal thing in his life now. While everyone around him rushed downhill to la-la land, he could rely on Tammy to understand him. She came from a different background, where religion lost the battle a long time ago to common sense and logic.

"You know that my dad didn't speak with Nir for almost two years... I never told you why. I was ashamed of it, and at the same time afraid of it..."

Tammy nodded. She looked at him, her gaze warm and comforting.

"Two years ago, when Nir was waiting to join the army, he hung around with some friends. One of them asked Nir to replace him on a school trip as a paid chaperone. A trip with third graders to the Weizmann Science Institute. I think Nir helped his friend because of that, not the money. He loved science. He always built things—machines, electronics. On the way back their bus driver lost control, and the bus rolled over."

"I remember it from the news!" Tammy raised her hand to her mouth, her eyes wide. "Nir was on that bus? Poor guy!" She moaned.

"Yes, but he was one of the lucky ones. He didn't end up in critical condition or suffer any long-term injuries. Only," Ram did the air quotes, "*only* PTSD. After that, the army did not think twice. They wouldn't even let him volunteer for the most mundane role, and they dismissed him. Nir was devastated. He looked forward to his service, and that door was shut off, forever.

"And then there was this woman."

Tammy thought it was about a woman. Now she knew for sure.

"Rachel Tabackman. She was one of the parents who accompanied the school class for the trip. Her son was a bright kid, or so the newspapers said. He sat with a friend at the front of the bus, while she was sitting a few rows behind with another parent. Her son died instantly. He flew out of the window, and they found him on the road, fifty meters from where the bus landed.

"Rachel was not harmed much. She helped other kids out of the wreck when she saw Nir. He was unconscious. She was the one who saved him. Fire erupted on the bus, and she pulled him out. Another parent was outside of the bus, and together they hauled Nir away. She *saved* Nir's life."

Ram paused. He swallowed hard. Their family endured much pain and sorrow since his mother died.

"The emergency services came after a while," he continued, "taking the injured to the hospital and declaring the deaths. They sent Nir to Assaf Harofeh hospital. During the first week he was in and out of consciousness. The doctors said he didn't suffer any internal bleeding and no head trauma. His brain was not damaged. They couldn't explain why he continued to lose consciousness. My dad sat with him for hours. But he could not be there *all* the time. So I took his place when I could, and our aunt, Chava, helped us too.

"His condition improved after a week. The doctors wanted him to stay under surveillance for a few more nights. On the eighth day, Rachel Tabackman came to visit. She had just finished sitting *shiva* for her son. We didn't know she saved Nir from the bus. I found out much later. Nir told me about it one night, after—well, that came later. At the time, we only knew that she was with him on the bus and that she came to visit him at the hospital. We didn't ask too many questions. Other than her tired face and puffy eyes, she didn't seem like she was hurt in the accident. Losing a son is bad enough."

Ram looked at Tammy, his sadness reflected back in her eyes.

"Nir was happy to see her. Everything poured out—crying, retelling what happened, even laughing. She was the only one who put a smile back on his face. When he was finally released from the hospital, physically he was fine, but mentally—he just shut down. He would sit for hours in front of the TV, staring blindly at the moving pictures. Our dad was very upset. He didn't know how to handle Nir. Nir met with a psychologist. It was the only thing that seemed to help. The school, with the aid of the insurance company that insured the trip, set up the survivors with a hotline. And they met with them in person every other week. Abba drove him to these meetings.

"That is where he met Rachel again. After one of the meetings, she told our dad that she could drive Nir back home; she won't mind. My dad was happy to take her offer. He detested waiting outside for the sessions to be over. And she said she was going to the Tel Aviv area, anyway. After that, they started chatting on the phone and online. Nir was home alone for many hours, and no one truly knew how he passed the time. A lot of it was spent online with her.

"One thing led to another, and they had an affair. Rachel was thirty-five, married, and had two kids, one alive. Her oldest one, Nati, died in the crash. Her husband often traveled on business—he worked in hi-tech, I think—and in Nir she found comfort and companionship. Nir would disappear for a few days. My dad was worried about him since Nir didn't bother telling him his whereabouts. But he always came back."

"But wait," Tammy interrupted him, "did he know Nir was seeing Rachel?"

Ram shook his head. "No, no one knew... we only found that later. He just disappeared for several days at a time. It happened a number of times. Abba returned to his old ways, trying to control Nir's activities—shouting, threatening. That was a sure way to drive Nir further away. I can't remember how long after the bus crash, but Nir packed his things one day and was gone for good. He left a note for my dad. In it he wrote, *I found someone with whom to live. She loves me. Goodbye.* That's it.

"At first, we didn't know where he was. I tried to contact him through his email and left messages with his friends. I asked them to tell Nir to call me when they heard from him. But no one did. After almost a week he called me. I scolded him for not returning my emails, for not being in touch. I literally freaked out on him... He asked me to meet him. I had to get a pass from the army, and I arranged to leave that evening. We met in a mall, not far from Netanya, on the highway to Haifa.

"When I saw him, he looked happy, euphoric almost. I hadn't seen him happy like that for a very long time. Probably since before my imma passed away. He cut to the chase quickly, not bothering with apologies for his disappearance.

"'You have heard from Abba that I left,' he said, 'and the note I left him.'

"'Yes,' I said. 'Who is she?' I was upset and curious at the same time.

"'Rachel Tabackman.'

"'The woman from the accident? What do you mean? She is married, she has a kid...' I didn't comprehend what he was saying.

"'She loves me, and I love her, and that's all that matters. No one has ever loved me like that. She is going to leave her husband and be with me...'

"I didn't believe what I was hearing. Was this part of the shock Nir and Rachel endured since the crash? They were both injured, and they found solace in each other. But still...

"'She is much older than you Nir. And has a family... Would you want her to leave her husband for you?' I asked.

"'She said this is stronger than anything; she cannot control it; she has never felt like this in her life.'

"'I don't get it, Nir. I really don't.' As much as I tried being patient and understanding, I just couldn't get the attraction they had. The entire situation was just off. 'And what about Abba and Millie? How will you tell them?'

"'They will find out sooner or later. You don't have to tell them anything, just that you saw me and I am okay.'

"'Easy for you to say,' I said. Still, not grasping what Nir was doing, I kept pushing, 'But why? There are hundreds of young girls you can meet—unattached, no kids, no mess with husbands, no broken families. Why *this* woman?'

Nir only looked at me. Then he said, 'She saved my life.'

"He then told me the rest of the story. How she was looking for her son, Nati, in the wreck. And she couldn't find him. She found Nir unconscious but still breathing. She pulled him to safety. Without her he would have been left on the bus and died in the fire. It was stronger than both of them. I didn't protest anymore, not that I liked the situation.

"After that, I didn't see Nir for about three months. He sent me a short email two days after we met. He told me that he and Rachel had moved, but he didn't say where to. They were happy, deeply in love. He didn't mention her kid in the email. I learned later that she brought him with her. He asked me to explain it to Abba and Millie. That he didn't mean to hurt anyone. He needed time away, and he was in love."

Ram took a long break. He wasn't accustomed to telling long stories. Tammy offered to bring him a cup of tea from the kitchen, which he accepted. He needed time to think through the rest of the story.

Tammy returned from the kitchen, carrying a mug of steaming nana-mint tea in one hand and a package of lemon-flavored wafers in the other. "Your aunt Chava is so adorable!" she said. "She fussed around, helping me find where things are."

"Yes, that is Chava," Ram said. He sipped the hot liquid, cherishing the aroma of the fresh nana-mint leaves. "Thanks."

"If the rest of your family is like her, I wouldn't see why it would be a problem for you to tell them about our relationship." Tammy sat down next to him, folding her legs under her.

"You don't know them."

Tammy only nodded, patiently waiting for him to continue his tale. She opened the pack of wafers, offering him first.

"So I had to do the dirty work, telling my dad about Nir living with her. That is probably the one thing I will never be able to forgive Nir for making me do. Now it's too late anyway, right?

"It was *terrible*. He is such a proud man, my dad, but for all the wrong reasons. He shouted and cursed. All he cared about was what his friends would say; how he would look at them when he saw them at the synagogue, what they would say behind his back. How happy he was that Imma was not alive to have to live through this, saying she was turning in her grave... He didn't ask me how Nir was doing, or whether there is anything we could do to help him. He was lamenting about Nir's waste of time, about the family Nir broke... Nothing I said would make him see things differently. Honestly, I think he didn't hear most of what I said. He was so angry!"

"Did you tell him that she saved Nir in the accident?" Tammy asked.

"I did. But by that time he completely shut down. He said he didn't want to speak about it anymore. Didn't want to hear about Nir or talk about him. He wanted me to cut off any communication I had with Nir. He wanted Millie to do the same."

"How did Millie take it?"

"I spoke to her later that night. She cried a lot and was devastated, but mostly that Nir wasn't around. She didn't care about all the rest. She wanted him to be closer. She loved him very much. When I told her about our dad's reaction, all she said was, 'I am not surprised.' She is a quiet one, our little sister, but she is very smart…"

Tammy shifted uncomfortably in her seat.

"After that," Ram went on, "Nir would send me emails once a week or so. He wrote that he was well. He never said exactly where he was staying; he mentioned an old aunt of Rachel's and a room in her house. It was always vague. It's not like we would come and force him back home with a gun to his head, right? But that's how he was. Once, he attached to the email a picture of himself and Rachel, the background behind them looks like a desert, maybe in the Negev. And they smiled at the camera. They looked happy.

"I didn't ask him too many questions. I told him about Abba's reaction, and his refusal to talk about Nir. I think it hurt Nir enormously, but he never complained about it. In the beginning he wrote that he called Abba, and his calls were never answered. Then he didn't mention it again. I don't know if he tried again to reach out to Abba, not back then, anyway. He was just like Abba—stubborn and proud. He always finished his letters with kisses and asked me to tell Abba and Millie that he loves them.

"The emails continued, although not at the same rate and enthusiasm as in the beginning. About three months later, I got a call at my office. The *Shin Gimel* on duty at the base's entrance told me a civilian guy was waiting for me at the front gate. He wouldn't tell her his name, she said, but he looked similar to me. My heart leaped. I dashed outside of the office, down the administration building and the barracks, and through the main road to the gate. Nir was waiting for me outside."

Ram stopped again, breathing heavily as if he just finished that run to the gate post. Drinking his tea, he focused on the leaves floating inside. Their color changed to a dark brown.

"He came back home, he said. Things didn't work out. She couldn't handle both him and her kid. They started fighting and were angry at each other all the time. Their deep love turned into a nasty match of accusations and bitterness. She stayed behind, or returned to her husband. I don't really know. Nir was back, and now he didn't know what he would do, where he would live. He couldn't go back to our dad's place. It would be too dreadful to deal with Abba after the way he reacted to Nir's adventure. For Nir, going there was out of the question.

"He stayed with me for three days, but that could not have been a long-term arrangement. He liked being in the *merkaz*, with the hustle and bustle of Tel Aviv life. And my life in the army made him restless. I think he was jealous, although he never said anything about it. We talked about his options. I convinced him that he must try to go back to school, learn something productive, something he can do with his life. He would have to work hard and find jobs to finance his studies and a place to live.

"In the end, I lent him some money, rent for a couple of months. He rented a room in Tel Aviv with two other guys. He then found some odd jobs. He never complained, and he paid back the loan pretty quickly."

"Sounds like he was back on his feet," Tammy said.

"Yes. I think he learned from that experience; he matured and grew. He told me once he realized that if he won't take care of himself, no one would."

"And your father? Why didn't he talk to Nir after the affair ended?"

"At first, Nir asked me not to tell our dad that he is back. He didn't want any favors or to be pitied. When he settled down after he had rented the room and was working, more or less, I persuaded him that I would tell Abba. I hoped our dad would see now that he can get off his tall tree. Oh, how wrong I was. He was even more stubborn, climbing even higher on that tree. If mom were alive, she would have known how to get him off his high place. She always did. But I failed. Nir was not surprised. On the contrary, I thought he was relieved. But now I doubt it… In the few times I have seen him since, he always seemed sad, depressed even.

"I think he missed our dad, and because of his stupid pride, he didn't say it."

CHAPTER 14

CHAIM

I didn't know! Oh, my dear God, what have I done? What have I done!

I didn't know she was the one who saved Nir. The one who dragged him out of the wreck. Her child died in that horrible accident, and she was selfless enough to help my son, my Niri.

She saved his life.

A nauseating wave crashes forcefully on the rock of my heart. My stomach turns and flips, and my heart sinks deep to meet it. I think I am going to vomit, or faint, or both. Is losing consciousness even possible in this place?

She saved his life, and I didn't know, and I shut him away, and I didn't talk with him, and now he is dead, dead, *dead*, and I miss him. I miss him so much…

Flashes of thoughts and questions pass through my exhausted mind, like piercing lightning in the darkness of my consciousness. Feelings trail behind them, raw and immediate, punching me from within, blinding me with their aggressive colors.

Why has no one told me? Dark red *anger.*

Maybe someone did and I didn't listen. Ram had said so much and I was buried in my own world. Blotches of dirty purple *confusion* mixed with ugly gray *shame.*

If Nir only said that the only reason he was alive is because of her, I would have understood it, been more accepting. Deep indigo *sorrow.*

But would I? She was married. With a kid. He broke that family. Blinding yellow *righteousness.*

But Nir, he was my son, my beloved son! Black. Black *agony.*

I find myself on my knees, my forehead on the ground, my hands covering my head, my body rolling into a ball. Dry tears cover my face, my knuckles are bleeding. I hold the little stone so tight in my grip that it stamped its shape into my palm.

My fingers are sore, but I can't let it go. Not yet.

I slowly raise my head to look around.

The bus wreckage is still here. It looks flat, like a huge cartoon—the dark areas are as black as coal, the highlights like splashes of white paint, the middle tones broken into shapes, framed in black outlines. Tongues of fire arise from the vehicle's front quarters. These, too, look unreal—artificial, cold flames. Smoke engulfs the cartoonish bus, filling the space between us.

I panic. I must move away before I choke to death. I stand up too quickly, my head swirling, and I stumble down, nearly falling flat on my face. Blood pulses through my temples. I hold my breath.

The smoke doesn't smell! Inhaling the fluffy gray substance doesn't bother my breathing at all. My eyes don't burn nor tear. *Fog.* It's fog coming out of a fog machine, like on a stage in the theater or concerts.

I rise again, slowly this time, careful not to rush it. My eyes focus and my vision clears. I see now why the bus looks flat and the fire unreal. It's a theater set. I'm standing in the middle of an enormous stage. Behind me is the make-believe body of a crashed bus. The fake fire is made of red, orange, and yellow streamers attached to the floor, fluttering and flapping in the air by an unseen fan under the stage. Machines spread white fog behind the bus.

A scene unfolds in front of me. The mutilated bodies of the dead kids, the source of the blood streams around me, are still there. But now they are lifeless dummies, made of plastic and painted red. Dark scarlet paint covers the floor in an intricate design. In the reflection of lights, some areas look wet. A confetti of clear flat plastic bits replaced the shattered glass, scattered around the bodies, over and across where the bus lies on its roof. Spotlights are mounted on brackets in the high ceiling. They shine in different directions, dramatically illuminating the scene below. The shadows are deep and dark. The highlights are bright and striking.

A rumble of voices starts. At first they are low, hard to hear and understand. Then they grow louder, stronger, more and more voices. Crying kids. Kids in pain. Kids begging for their mothers. Kids yelling to stop the hurting, to turn off the lights, to make it go away. *Take the pain away, Imma. Don't let the bad man come closer, Abba.*

I press my palms hard against my ears, trying to block out the voices. It's useless.

At the corner of my eye, I notice a movement. I turn my head, but all is still. I wait for some time. There, a body of a small boy, his eyes wide open, looking my way. His lower body twists and turns the other way, legs sprawled. Two bright dots are painted at the corner of his eyes. Tears. A master artist created this life-like face, and now it gnaws at me.

The cries are still around me, but among them I hear another voice, a chant. An angelic voice rises quietly to comfort the agonized children.

My heart is in you,
I'm here with you,
I live for you.
My child,
My child,
My child.

My gaze is fixed on the black circles painted for the little boy's eyes. Suddenly, the boy's back lifts from the floor, jerking the lifeless little body, hands and legs slumped on all four corners. The head falls violently, his hair brushing the ground. I take a step back. The little body twitches and stirs as if an invisible giant holds it in its palm and jerks it forcefully. Then, slowly, the dummy boy's torso rises from the floor. It continues floating up toward the lights above, followed by its midsection and legs. The head tilts and rolls from side to side, all the while its dotted eyes are wide open, the little tears shining in the spotlight.

From the birth of you,
I was there for you,
Because I am you.
My child,
My child,
My child.

Another body of a little girl jerks on the floor, first the upper body rising, followed by the bottom and legs. Her long golden hair sweeps the floor, and then it's her only body part that touches the floor. Five more seconds and the hair, too, is airborne. Then another small girl, and then all the bodies float in the air. Heads tilt to one side and roll to the other, eyes wide open, with astonishing looks refusing to believe what happened to them. Others have their eyes closed, their faces a calm mask. They continue their ascent to the ceiling on invisible strings.

As they rise, the children hush, cease their crying. The dark skies in the ceiling welcome these pure angels into their fold. The angelic voice continues its song,

I've gone from you,
The pain of you,
The loss by you.
My child,
My child,
My child.

When they are midway between earth and heaven—
Is this what I'm supposed to see? To think?
—each child grows a set of wings. White beautiful wings come out of their backs, spreading magnificently behind them, filling the air around them. Their shadows on the floor create an intricate pattern of wings, legs, and arms, interlocked, one emerging from the other, like an Escher painting.

There are tears in the air,
Some of joy, others of pain,
They are washing like rain.
My child,
My child,
My child.

I squint to see better into the high ceiling above. It has deep dark recesses. The bodies rise, each one fits snugly into one of these recesses. One of the dolls doesn't go all the way up. It is stuck in its track, suspended between floor and ceiling, heaven and earth. While the rest of the kids slowly disappear into the darkness above, a lonely angel boy is left behind. Its body is intact, the face white as chalk, the eyes closed. No evidence shows what injury had killed him.

The music stops. A shuffling noise comes from what I think to be backstage. I hear footsteps and something being dragged around. Then I see who makes these noises.

Nir appears from behind the bus, close to the suspended angel boy. He pulls behind him a long aluminum ladder. A utility belt is attached to his hip, the red and yellow handles of the tools sticking out. Nir drags the ladder under the boy. He unfolds and adjusts it to the proper height, then secures it to the floor on its rubber feet. He climbs the rungs until he reaches the level of the dummy angel. Using the tool from his belt, Nir detaches the dummy from the apparatus it is hanged from. He then carries it carefully down the ladder and lays it on the floor.

Nir is working on the boy. He sometimes obstructs my view, crouching on his knees between the plastic angel and me. But when he turns around to the other side I can see him arranging and rearranging the doll. He squeezes paint onto a white plate and with small brushes he touches the colors of the boy's face and arms. Next, he sets the tools, paints, and brushes aside, and with a soft bristle hair brush, similar to the one Sarah used to brush the kids' hair when they were babies, he lovingly cleans the feathers of the white wings. He spends a long time painstakingly caring for the boy. Finally, Nir must be satisfied with the results, as he puts down the little brush next to the other tools. He stands up, turns around, and starts walking in my direction.

I am not sure what to expect. The entire experience of seeing Nir, from the beach to the synagogue, the *yeshiva* dorm, Sarah's hospital room, and then the bus accident site—none of it follows a normal logic. I resolve to stand there and wait.

He comes closer, looking directly at me as he walks. When he reaches me, Nir raises his hands in request motion, pointing at what I am holding. He looks at it. I finally look as well. The model airplane is in my hand. His first airplane, the one glued together from hundreds of broken pieces. The one his second-self gave me at the last dorm room. He wants it now.

I hold it out with both hands, like an offering. He touches the plane with the tips of his fingers, a gentle touch. His hands are spotted with white and yellow paint. I can feel his eyes staring at me. I can't let go of the little airplane. I want to hold on to it and never let it go.

Our fingertips nearly touch each other from both ends of the cylindrical form. I can almost feel his pulse through the warm surface.

"Thank you, Abba," he says and nods gently.

My eyes meet his eyes. I let go of the little plane.

Nir turns, taking the airplane with him to the little angel. With a couple of quick strokes, he somehow attaches the airplane to the boy's hands. The boy's plastic head is tilted down to look at what its plastic hands are holding. The expression changes on its shiny artificial face. Its closed eyes and mouth are smiling. For a moment he does not look like a plastic dummy, rather a real boy, dreaming a sweet dream, smiling in its sleep.

Picking him up in both hands, Nir carries the angel boy up the ladder and attaches him back to the brackets he was hanged from. He secures the boy and checks one last time that everything is in place. Satisfied, Nir descends down the ladder and returns the way he came, dragging the ladder behind him.

When he is out of sight, the lights dim slowly until the stage is dark again. One spotlight shines on the single angel boy, and the music starts again.

I am waiting for you,
We will be together,
It will be forever.
My child,
My child,
My child.

The angel boy ascends to its heavenly position in the ceiling.
The music ends.
The single spotlight shuts off.
The show is over.

CHAPTER 15

Wednesday, Fourth Day of the Shiva

RAM

The next morning a few of Ben-Israel's friends attended the *shiva* house for *Shacharit*, the morning service. Even without their leader amongst them, the small group of followers stayed together throughout the service, eyeing Chaim like a flock of gosling eye their mother.

The thought that their home has become a center for Kabbalah worshipers unnerved Ram. Chaim, on the other hand, was happy to see them. He loved the special attention. Ram felt a buzz of excitement in the air, filling the space in the apartment. He did not like it for one bit.

During the *Shmone Esre*, in the second blessing of the daily prayer, Chaim chanted loudly,

"*Vene'eman ata le'hachayot metim*": And You are trustworthy to resurrect the dead.

"*Baruch ata Adonai Mechaye Hametim*": Blessed are You, Lord, who resuscitate the dead.

When *Shacharit* was over, while the men folded their *tefillin* and prayer shawls, Chaim barely held back his excitement.

"He came again last night," he said to the Ben-Israelites.

"The Resurrector?" one of them asked. "Was he here again?" He dropped the half-folded *tallit* on the chair on top of a blue velvet *tallit* bag. The gold-threaded name embroidered on the bag identified him as Gilad.

"No, no." Chaim waved his hand. "Nir! I saw Nir again last night."

"Oh," Gilad said. He picked his *tallit* from the chair and continued folding it. His friends echoed his movements, each one focusing on their own religious artifacts.

Ram stayed quiet. *I hoped this would pass,* he thought. *Abba's 'sightings,' 'seeing' Nir and 'speaking' to him. What good can come from this?* he wondered. *And this gang, they don't care at all for Chaim and his rendezvous with Nir. All they want is their elusive* Mekubal, *their Eliyahu Hanavi…* Ram caught himself mid thought: *Believing Abba's claims of seeing Nir would put me in with these nut-jobs.* He felt a headache building up behind his eyes.

Chaim sat down, and Ram sat next to him. Chava brought a tray from the kitchen with their breakfast: white bread sliced into thick pieces, cottage cheese, and a plate of cut vegetables—cucumbers, tomatoes, green pepper, olives. Another dish contained egg salad. Chaim washed his hands in the basin that stood nearby, wiped them with a towel, and said the blessings—for washing the hands, for the bread. He bit into a slice of bread so he could continue talking.

"He was on a stage building a theater set," he said.

Ram looked up, alert, listening to his father. *How does Abba know?*

Chaim spread some cheese on the bread and covered it with two slices of cucumber.

"There was a scene with dummy dolls," he continued, "boys and girls. They moved around the stage, flew up in the air, grew beautiful white wings, and turned into angels. Then one of them got stuck in mid-air, and Nir came and fixed it."

What? How is that possible? Ram thought. *Who told Abba about Nir's last job?* Nir worked at a small community theater.

He had great hands and could build anything. He taught himself mechanics and electronics, and what he didn't know, he learned on the job.

At the theater, he built sets and constructed special effects. The job was perfect for him. He told Ram about his co-workers and the theater crew, the actresses and directors—they were artistic and creative, yet narcissistic and control freaks. Nir did not mind. He was good at what he did, he learned on the job, and he was happy. But Chaim did not know about the job, at least not from Ram. Even if Ram intended to tell him, Chaim never wanted to listen. *Maybe someone else told him? He might have known all along and never said anything... His pride won't let him admit it to anyone! This would not be the first time...*

But the details... Nir never mentioned props like kids that became angels. Of course, it was possible that Ram didn't know all the sets and props Nir worked on. Nir told him about his work, plays and musicals they produced. It was possible that he missed some.

Chaim continued relaying his story to the small group around him. The Ben-Israelites absorbed every word, adding another story to the growing collection glorifying the power of their *Mekubal*.

When Chaim completed the tale, he fell silent. He sat quietly for several minutes, his eyes half closed. No one interrupted his quiet contemplation.

***

The morning proceeded in a nerve-wrecking slowness, following the sun on her lazy ascend. Men and women came and left. Ram was not surprised that the Ben-Israelites group size didn't dwindle much. Some of them left, replaced by others, but throughout the pre-lunch hours they kept their presence.

At one time, Ram and Chaim had a semi-private moment, while their visitors were either engaged in small talk with each other or were scouring the food trays at the dining table.

"The girl, what was her name?" Chaim broke the silence, looking at Ram.

"Which girl?" Ram asked.

"The redhead, pretty one. She was here yesterday, came for you. Didn't she stay until late?"

"Tammy?" *Why does he ask about Tammy now?*

"Yes, yes, Tammy. Such a nice girl," Chaim said.

"She is nice, yes."

Nice. Nice could mean so many things when it came from his dad. It could mean he genuinely liked her. Ram was worried it actually meant the opposite. That his father said "nice" to mask the fact he did not like her at all. *And when exactly did Abba have the opportunity to talk with her and assess her? And yet, "nice" is okay. Safe. But where does he go from here?*

"She seems like a good person. I don't know, something about her... maybe it's her eyes? Wise and understanding..." Chaim continued. "Where is she from?"

Getting into Tammy's background was a sure way to disaster.

"I know her from the army. We work together," Ram replied.

"Right, right. But where is she from originally? Where did she grow up?"

"She is from Kibbutz Beit Kama." Ram squirmed in his seat. *Let him stop there and not ask any further, please!*

"Beit Kama? Where is that?"

"It's in the northern Negev, maybe twenty minutes from Be'er Sheva."

"That's nice…" Chaim's eyes glazed over, unfocused. "And… do you love her?" Chaim asked.

Not a question about her Kibbutz. Worse. Ram felt the air knocked out of his lungs. He blushed, lost for words. Since when had his father become so observant? And so blunt? They *never* discussed relationships, not to mention the L word. It was completely out of character.

"Oh, don't be shy, Ram. I saw how she looked at you. And how you were happy to see her. I have eyes, you know."

Millie appeared from the depths of the house. She sat down on the low sofa next to Ram. She was quiet, clutching her prayer book with both hands.

Ram hesitated. He should tell the truth and be done with it, let it all come out. He breathed heavily. He wasn't ready yet. "She is a good friend," Ram finally said. "We work together."

Chaim looked at him, not pursuing the matter further. He turned to Millie.

"You believe me, right Millie-li?" he asked.

"About Nir?" she asked. "If you say so, Abba, I believe you. I wish I could see him myself…" Her eyes were red. "I miss him so much."

Chaim reached out to hug her. An awkward hug. "Me too," he said. "Me too."

Another atypical first, Ram thought. *Where was he for the last two years? It's too late now that Nir is dead,* he wanted to shout.

Instead, he kept quiet.

Once Millie calmed down a bit, she opened her prayer book and started reading a prayer. Her lips moved soundlessly. Chaim's attention was back on Ram.

"So, listen," he said. "If Tammy comes back, don't hide her in your room again. She can sit with us here, okay?"

Ram nodded. *Sure. Fine.*

Millie, on hearing this, raised her head in surprise from her prayer book. With a look of dismay on her face, she stopped her chanting mid-way.

***

Ben-Israel joined them when the sun was high in the sky. He was accompanied by a new face, someone who wasn't there before but whose face they all knew. It was the mayor.

Chaim and Ram were surprised to see him. For Chaim, this was another validation that he was not going crazy and that a similar experience had happened to other people before him. For Ram, on the other hand, it was another nail in his father's strange-behavior-coffin. Deranged settlers-hilltop-youth, crazy politicians—they were all the same. Put them separately and they each stir the pot. Put them together—they become fire that burns the dish.

"Please, please, come. Sit with us," Chaim invited the elderly mayor.

The mayor, used to people fussing around him, sat in a chair close to Chaim.

"I am so sorry for your loss," he said, addressing Chaim first, then Ram. "It must be a terrible time for you. How old was she?"

Ram looked at his father. Would he correct the mayor?

Chaim didn't seem to notice. "Almost twenty-one. His birthday would have been the next Rosh Hashanah."

"What a shame, such a young age." The mayor looked around him and noticed Nir's framed photo on the table next to the memorial candle. "Such a handsome fellow." Like any good politician, the mayor corrected himself, unfazed by his earlier slip-up.

Chaim sat at the edge of the sofa. His body coiled like a spring, about to be released at any moment. "So, you came all the way to visit us," he said. "I have heard from Mr. Ben-Israel that—"

"It's nothing, really. I... how should I say it..." the mayor said, a painful look on his face. "I had a vision." The last word came out as merely a whisper.

He has a hard time saying it out loud, Ram thought.

Chaim nodded, encouraging the mayor silently, comradery weaving seamlessly between them.

The mayor looked around, checking who else was tuned into the discussion. The room was quiet, everyone in attendance had their eyes on him. He scratched his neck with the rough skin of his thumb.

"Hmm, can we talk in private?" he finally asked.

"Of course!" Chaim jumped off the sofa, the tension released from his body into action. "Let's go to the kitchen."

Ram would not let the exchange happen in his absence. He rose to follow them. Although the mayor shot him a glance, he did not object. He followed Chaim, sandwiched between father and son. Several moans of disappointment came from the people sitting behind them.

"I had a vision," the mayor said as they entered the dark abandoned kitchen. "A vision of a loved one who passed away. The details don't matter. And... well, things didn't end up like I expected them to, like I *wished* they would have. I messed up. Not only the first opportunity, but also my second chance." He paused.

Chaim lowered his eyes, looking at his hands. Did Ram see them shake? The hands that always seemed sure of their grip now held each other tight like they were afraid to separate.

"I wish I could change things," he said in a low voice, barely audible.

"I want another chance, one last time," the mayor said.

"Why did you come here?" Ram blurted. He could not hold his anger any longer. "Why do you even think you can get this second chance here?" The last words spat out with contempt.

Chaim didn't stir on Ram's outburst.

"I came to ask you for a favor," the mayor addressed Chaim. He looked old and tired, his eyes recessed deeply in his face. He ignored Ram, his voice urgent. "If the *Mechaye* comes here again, ask him to come to me, or call me, and I will come anywhere he wants. I will pay him any amount he is asking for, tell him. If you don't see him but still see your son, see if he can find my..." he hesitated. "My... my daughter," he finally said.

"Your daughter?"

"Find my Dafna and tell her I need to see her again. In the same place where she always waited for me after *Mechaye Hametim* brought her back to me."

"Do you think they can see each other?" Chaim asked, raising his eyes for the first time to look at the mayor.

The mayor took out an old photograph from his jacket's inner pocket. "This is her, my Dafna. She is thirteen in the picture. She was taken from us two weeks before her fourteenth birthday."

Chaim took the picture. He passed a slow finger over the face staring at him. "Beautiful," he said.

"Fourteen years ago. There isn't a day that I don't think about her. You might have heard that my wife and I are separated. She never believed that I saw Dafna, that the *Mechaye Hametim* was, *is*, real. She called me crazy.

Claimed I was talking to myself, chanting to empty rooms. I believed her sometimes. I felt I was dozing in and out of reality." He paused for a few seconds. "I tried to save my marriage," he continued, "and I tried to save my dear girl's soul, and I failed in both."

Now everything the mayor needed to say was out in the open. His shoulders dropped heavily, and he looked ancient. "Okay," he said. "I had taken up enough of your time."

"But is it possible?" Chaim asked.

When the mayor blinked at him, as if he just woke up from a deep sleep without recollection of where he was, Chaim asked again, more forcefully, "Is it possible to save them? Can I save Nir? Can you save your daughter?"

The mayor shrugged his shoulders. "I believe in our mighty God, and with Him—everything is possible."

With that, he turned around and left the kitchen, leaving a stunned Ram and contemplating Chaim behind.

***

TAMMY

Tammy arrived again before lunchtime. She planned to return up north that evening and wanted to spend more time with Ram. Spending the night with Ram at his father's apartment was out of the question, so she stayed overnight with a friend from the kibbutz who moved to Tel Aviv.

When she entered the apartment, Ram was surrounded by a group of young men, all wearing knitted *kippahs*. Some had the tassels of their *tzitzit* hung low from under their shirts. She didn't know any of them. Ram sat relaxed on the sofa; he seemed in ease amongst them. Must be his childhood friends from the *yeshiva*. She leaned on a wall not far from the kitchen entrance, observing them quietly.

A heavyset guy, sitting on the edge of his seat with his back to her, was roaring to the group. "And now, Tomer is a father! Can you believe this schmuck has a kid of his own?"

Laughs erupted.

"He is not the first one with a kid, Motta," another young man said. "Homski has a girl, and Sapir has a boy. And I have heard that three more are expecting." He counted on his fingers. "Giat, Weinstein and Har-Dov."

"You are talking about babies, and our friend here," Motta pointed at Ram, "does not even have a girlfriend yet!"

Ram waved at him with his hand in dismissal while his friends continued their laughing and teasing.

Tammy felt a lump growing in her throat.

"*Shalom*. I'm Chaim."

Tammy jerked around.

"Oh, I'm sorry. I didn't mean to surprise you," Chaim said. He came from the kitchen, holding a steaming coffee mug. The mug declared that he was the "Best Abba."

"Oh, hi. I didn't see you," Tammy said, her hands smoothing an invisible crease in her blouse.

"It's okay. Come, let's find a seat." He led her to a couple of chairs and sat down on one of them, waiting for her to join him. "This is actually refreshing. I'm already tired of that awful sofa. It's so uncomfortable and hard to get up without the cushions. I think I'll buy a new one after this—" he gestured around him, "is all over."

Tammy smiled.

"And you know what else is refreshing?"

She shook her head.

Now it was his turn to smile. "That I took my coffee all by myself, no one serving me food! And that you did not scold me for sitting on a regular chair!"

Tammy was not sure she followed. Her confused look made Chaim laugh.

"It's okay," he reassured her. "It's actually, for once, a good thing."

Tammy made a mental note to ask Ram about it later.

"So, Ram told me you are from Kibbutz Beit Kama. Were you born there?"

So he spoke to his father about me. That's good. How much, though, did he say?

"Yes, I am third-generation in Beit Kama. My grandparents were one of the founders."

"That's wonderful! I think what's his name was from Beit Kama. What was it? The *Kova Tembel* robber? I can't remember his name…"

Tammy knew who he was talking about. There were a few famous generals, special unit fighters, a former head of the Mossad, and a minister, all from her kibbutz. But people seemed to remember the *Kova Tembel* robber, especially people on the opposite side of the political scale. The *Kova Tembel* robber was a rather stupid nickname dubbed by the media to a guy who robbed eleven bank branches around the Negev, all while wearing work coveralls, a bandana covering his mouth and nose, and a khaki bucket hat, a *Kova Tembel*—a tembel, Hebrew for idiot—on his head.

"Yes, that's right." She smiled thinly. "Dan Spiegel."

"Exactly!" Chaim exclaimed, excited to remember the name. "Dan Spiegel. So what happened to him?"

Tammy didn't follow the tabloids nor the internal intrigues of the kibbutz. "I am not sure," she finally said. "Probably in jail."

"Good, good." He sipped his hot coffee slowly and said, "And you and Ram, is it serious?"

He liked to change subjects, she noticed. She found it confusing but also refreshing in a way. He gave the same attention to both gossip and serious matters. Maybe it was his way to process harder-to-approach topics; diverting to safer terrains, then coming back to the tough ones. But he still caught her by surprise.

"Yes," she said. *Oh, what the hell,* she thought. *He will find out at the end, anyway. This is for the best.* She smiled, the little freckles on her cheeks raised high below her eyes.

Chaim smiled back. A small, narrow crook of his mouth.

"How was your childhood in the kibbutz? Did you live with your parents or with all the kids?" He changed the subject again.

Tammy was not sure where this line of questions is leading. Or maybe it didn't lead anywhere.

"I had a childhood nanny in the kibbutz," Tammy said. "Her name was Shosh."

"I figured," Chaim said, a hint of judgment in this brief statement.

"It was a wonderful childhood," Tammy said, gently. If she had to, she could defend the way of her upbringing, with all its problems and, to some, experimental qualities. But she didn't want to do it right then.

"You know," Chaim looked directly into her eyes, a hard, searching gaze. "I was also raised by a stranger woman after my mother left us."

Tammy shook her head. "No, I didn't know." How would she? She wasn't sure Ram knew. He had never mentioned it.

"Yes, our neighbor. She cooked for us and cleaned our home for several years, until my father remarried."

"And what happened to your mother?" More than she was shocked by Chaim's childhood misfortune, Tammy was surprised that he opened up to her and told her about it.

"She left us!" Chaim rose his voice, almost shouting. Several people around them glanced in his direction. "My sister and I," he lowered his voice. "I was barely four years old, and Chava was one."

Tammy felt an urge to reach out and put her hand on Chaim's. To comfort him for the pain he seemingly harbored for most of his life. As she leaned forward in her chair, Chaim straightened up, keeping his distance from her.

"I am so sorry," Tammy said. She wasn't sure what she felt sorry about. The way she almost broke the religious rules of interaction between men and women? Chaim's recent loss? Or the child in him who lost his mother so many years ago?

"I know what it means to lose someone who is dear to you," she finally said. "Someone you love so much. Shosh was like the mother I needed. While my mother was always busy with the *common good*," she drew air quotes, "working in the cowshed, or the kibbutz's kitchen, or the date orchards, Shosh was the one who raised me. She died a few years ago... I miss her every day since."

Chaim sipped his coffee, but his eyes never left her. They had a strange mixture of warmth and chillness. On one hand, his gaze reminded her of Ram's eyes, but she also saw in them a cold calculating quality, as if he tried to penetrate her external layer and peer into her mind.

"Every day I wish I could see her again. I want to tell her about my happy moments, my difficult ones. Just to share my life with her."

Chaim nodded. Tammy searched in his eyes for any sign that she should stop what she was about to say, but she saw none.

"But it's not possible. I'm not a kid anymore. I know she is dead. She comes to me sometimes at night, in my dreams... These are the sweetest dreams, and I always want them to last forever. Brief visions of her, passing by on her way somewhere, or longer encounters; it doesn't matter. When I wake up, I always know it's just a dream..."

"Do you believe in life after death?" Chaim asked.

"I don't know. I never saw a proof for it, or one against it, so I just don't know."

"I used to believe in theory because it's part of our faith." Chaim drank the last drops of his coffee, then held the empty mug with both hands on his knee. "Our sages teach us that this world is a corridor for the next world. When my Sarah died, I prayed for her soul to rise and reach higher worlds, to enter heaven. But I must admit," he averted his eyes slightly, "it was very hard to feel it, *really* feel it.

"Now—" he paused, shaking his head, "I *actually* believe. Nir showed me. I can't prove it to anyone. It's not like I can take a camera and snap some pictures. Or a video. But I believe, no—I know!—that I see him. And *if* he's dead, it's only the body that is dead. His spirit and soul are still very much alive."

After a long pause, Chaim put the empty coffee mug down on the floor below his chair. Deep creases crossed his brow, and he looked like a man with a hard decision to make. Finally, he rubbed the top of his pants' pocket and said, "And, the place where I see him, it's not a dream. I have this—" his brow softened as he made up his mind, "I have this stone."

Chaim pushed a hand into his pocket and fished out a little object. Then, unceremoniously, he opened his palm. In the middle sat a little stone, not larger than an army "falafel," a major's rank insignia. Chaim looked at Tammy with new shine in his eyes.

When he saw the puzzled look on her face, Chaim closed his hand on the stone and quickly shoved it back into the depth of his pocket.

"Never mind, you won't understand," he mumbled.

"Try me."

Chaim looked her way suspiciously. "Well," he finally said, "the *Mechaye Hametim*, when he came here, he gave me this little stone, which was Nir's. I don't know how he got it, but I am one hundred percent certain it was Nir's. And I can use it to go into a—" he searched for the right word, "place—no, more like a state. And when I'm in that state, I see Nir. He is there, showing me things. So it's not a dream!"

Tammy looked at him, examined his face, the creases on his forehead and brow, the angles at both sides of his mouth, the redness in his eyes. What she believed she saw was a man who believed, without doubts, without shadows. But she also saw a religious person, a grieving father, a man who needed to make sense of what happened to him, to his family. And, maybe, a man who is losing his mind. But how can she judge him?

"I am not saying you are lying," she said. "You can see how this might be hard for some people to get, right?"

He nodded sadly.

"Hey, Tammy, you are back!" Ram finally noticed her. He jumped from his place on the sofa, ignoring his friends. His eyes squinted in worry.

"Yes, I am going back tonight, so I stopped by before I have to catch the bus," she said. "Your dad and I—"

"Had a great chat," Chaim finished her sentence. He got up, stretching his knees and lower back. "Here, you can sit with Tammy, or she can join us over there," he pointed at the sofa.

"We will go to my room," Ram said.

Chaim didn't wait for them to follow him to the sofa. He spotted some of his friends who just came through the door and settled back in his mourner's position.

***

When they reached his room, Ram asked, "Are you sure it was okay? What did he ask you? Did he grill you for information?"

"No, nothing like that." Tammy laughed. "He was really nice. Charming, actually. He wants you to believe him really badly—"

"About seeing Nir? Yeah, right."

"I'm worried for him, Ram. He believes this little stone—"

"It's nuts. Crazy religious mumbo jumbo!" Ram interrupted. "What did he ask about us?" he changed the subject.

"Just where I'm from, where we met… nothing much. He might surprise you, Ram."

"You don't know him! It's usually his way or the highway." Ram's voice rose. He was always anxious when talking about his father.

"Listen, Ram, you are not a kid anymore. You are a grown man making your own decisions, and you should stop worrying so much about hurting your father's feelings. You can't live in his shadow your entire life. It's not fair to you, and it's not fair to me."

Ram looked in her eyes. She tried to see what was behind them, what was going on in his head at that moment. He nodded, leaning his forehead against her, touching her lightly.

"When this is over, I will do something about it. I promise," he said.

That was good enough for her. For now.

CHAPTER 16

CHAIM

I stand in complete darkness in the center of the stage. The last music notes echo in my ears, and a negative image of the last angel boy is etched on my retina. I wait for something to happen. I don't know for how long: five minutes, or an hour. It all feels the same here. I should move, but it is too dark.

I could walk ahead in the darkness, but I may fall and break my neck. Nir will be here to show me the way, I am sure of that. If I am still here, and this... whatever this place is—this dimension—is real, it only means one thing: that I am still intended to see Nir. That this journey is not over.

I decide to sit down on the cold floor and wait.

After a while, I see a small light in the distance. It's moving, slightly twitching as it advances toward me. I cannot see what it is or how far it is from me. It grows as it approaches me in unusual movements—fast, zigzagging, fixing and adjusting its route to the general vicinity of my spot.

When the walking light closes the distance, I can finally recognize it. A crab! A little crab, walking sideways on eight hinged legs and carrying two uneven pincers ahead of its googly eyes. The light comes from within its flat body, it illuminates a circle around the little critter. Is this the same crab Nir was playing with at the Ashlag synagogue? It's the same size. The only light around me is the one coming from within the little thing, so it's hard to tell. If it is the same one, what is it doing here?

As if reading my mind, the little creature reaches me and stops beside my foot. It does not show any fear, just stands there, its big eyes staring both ways.

I rise to my feet. The closeness of the crab is unsettling. My looming size above it does not scare the crab away. On the contrary, it moves closer to me and pokes its right claw at the side of my shoe. My leg jerks reflexively, although I can't feel anything through the thick leather. The little rascal moves again toward my feet. It doesn't seem afraid that I would kick it. Poking me again gently, twice, it then quickly retreats.

When I don't move this time, it reaches me again, pokes me a few times, and draws back in the same direction it came from. After two meters, it turns around and waits.

Waits… It wants me to follow him. This is crazy. Follow him? A crab? It reminds me of a dog's behavior, not that I ever owned one, but I have seen it in the movies. But a crab? It cannot possibly come to me and ask me to follow it. How crazy is that?

But I *am* a bit crazy, aren't I? I saw my dead son and wife! I walked in this place and saw familiar buildings in all the wrong places… I saw kids doing despicable things, and they could not hear me… Music came from nowhere… Fish marked rooms… Dead bodies changed to dummy angels… So what would be so special about a little crab who acts like a dog?

I take one step toward the crab, directed by its light. Its little eyes are moving, and when it sees me coming its way, it turns around and moves a bit farther. I don't move, testing my theory. Would it come for me again? As if reading my mind, the crab returns toward me, waiting. If Nir is not here, maybe he sent that little creature to bring me along. What do I have to lose? I decide to follow it.

The crab walks at my pace. It doesn't hurry or rush me, nor does it lag behind. Its internal light is the only illumination I have. I am happy to do something, to follow someone, even if it is only a little crab. It is Nir's, I am sure of that.

It feels different under my feet. Instead of the hard and smooth floor of the stage, the ground is softer, surrendering under the pressure of my shoes, as if it is made of tiny particles, moving and grinding each other as I press them. Maybe I am walking on fine gravel or thick, coarse sand. It is impossible to see with the only light source moving in front of me, about twenty steps ahead. The terrain slopes mildly, first uphill, then rolling down. Still, there is no other source of light.

Everything around and above me is tar black.

The floor changes again. Now it mostly consists of pebble size rocks. Light from the little crab's belly highlights their smooth rounded shapes, reflected off their shiny surface. I hear the rocks crunch as I push them together with every step. The pebbles slide under me, and I struggle to stay on my feet.

"Wait," I say. Now I must have gone crazy, as I am talking to the little crab.

The little crab stops. It understood my demand.

I stumble until I reach my little guide, and in its light, I slowly lean down to examine the pebbles that the slippery ground is made of. They are similar to my—Nir's—little stone. Almost the same size and shape, each one is slightly different. There are many of them; however, I cannot see beyond the diameter of my guide's light.

I hold tighter to the little one in my hand. I must move on to a place that doesn't have other stones like it. Dropping mine here would mean one thing—that I will never find it amongst the other stones and will never make it back home. I can't lose it now.

So I rush on, letting the little crab pass by me on its tiny legs.

To my relief, the further we walk the larger the rocks grow. The challenge now is to find good footing, and I slow down to keep my balance. The darkness, on the other hand, is not as pitch black. A dim light falls around me, diffused to a thin glow. I can see where I am walking and find rocks large enough to step on. In the growing light, the crab's light diminishes to a tiny pulse at the heart of its hard shell body.

Where is the light coming from?

I finally see it. A small circle of light comes from above us, about three meters from the ground. A moonlight beam is peering through a hole in the wall. The crab wobbles sideways toward the light, moving up a sharp slope. A mound of boulders is stacked right below the hole, and the crab finds its way up, moving from one big rock to the next, climbing their vertical cliffs as naturally as walking on a flat surface. I hurry to him. The rocks are large enough for me to climb upon. I follow my little guide until I find myself face to face with the hole.

It is not as small as it looked from the distance. I peek through.

I see rows of houses, neatly standing side by side, the full moon low in the sky above them. They are all identical—one floor high, white walls, red terracotta slanted roofs, square windows, green doors. In the moonlight, their colors have a sickly hue, pale and anemic.

It would be easy enough to climb through that hole and out of the dark place I came from. As I look down beyond the jagged edge of the hole, my heart falls to my stomach. Directly below it—nothing, another dark space. Where is the ground?

The houses do not float in the air. They are rooted safely on a flat surface, a real street. They stand close together in two rows. The street between them is more like an alley, but still—there *is* an actual street, paved and tarred and, more importantly, a place I can walk on.

But directly below me, nothing.

The crab positions itself on the edge of the hole. It does not hesitate for a second. With one swift crab-like jump it leaps off the ledge and drops beyond it, into the darkness. As it falls, I notice something is written on its back. The crab's internal light glows through the letters. It spells one bright word.

Nir.

Now, what choice do I have? I wiggle through the hole in the wall, as it is large enough to fit my entire body comfortably. I am not as courageous as my little guide, so I pause for a few minutes, sitting on the rock at the opening. The crab fell below me, but from this distance, the details blur into one circle of light. It moves slowly toward the direction of the houses.

Feet first, I jump after the little creature.

I land in a splash. The cold water surprises me. Salty water engulfs me completely, pushing its way into my mouth, my nose, my eyes. I flail and kick helplessly, trying to reach the surface. I gulp for air. I panic. I must get hold of myself quickly. Otherwise, I will lose the crab with my son's name on its back, my only tour guide to this unknown territory. I cough up water as I try to make my way behind it. I reach down with my legs trying to feel for some solid ground, anything to stand on. After several failed attempts my tip-toes finally find the seafloor. I am in shallower waters. The waves at my back push me to the shore and help me ascend out of the water.

I finally exit the cold water. I fall to my knees, trying to catch my breath, coughing some more, shaking in my wet clothes. As my mind clears slowly from its recent flooding, I remember the little stone in my hand. Did I lose it? My hands wet, the sand sticks to them in an even layer. And yes, my right hand is closed shut. I squeeze it tighter, feeling the hard stone is still there. A loud gasp escapes my throat.

The little crab waits for me on the beach. It stands at the edge of the strip, where the developed urban scape starts. The houses I saw before from above are tall and eerie, towering above the little creature. The crab doesn't move as it waits for me to follow. It has a mission to complete. I hope its mission is to bring me to Nir.

When I reach the little crab, it starts moving again along the first row of houses. Narrow alleys cross the main street, perpendicular to the shore in neat rows of buildings. At the corner of each ally stands a thin pole, crowned by a blue sign, announcing their names: Ashlag Lane, Yeshiva Alley, Cancer Crescent, Crash Course, Angel Street. The crab scurries past each of them and stops only at the last one. It then turns to the right, where the narrow road curves away from the shoreline. The blue sign at the entrance to this small road is blank. The road has not yet been named.

What does it mean? It can't be a good sign. Chills run through my back, enhanced by my wet clothes.

I run after the crab. The houses on this street cling to each other in a long-jagged row. Graffiti covers every centimeter of the street level walls; huge green monsters and small spiky trolls, stars of David and the slogan proclaiming, "Death to the Arabs," illegible signatures of street "artists", and splashes of paint thrown haphazardly at every angle. Down the road a lone streetlamp spreads its narrow light beam, highlighting a small heap on the ground.

As I reach the streetlight, my stomach churns, the chills spreading up to my shoulders and my neck, and my teeth chatter. No, that can't be. I shut my eyes, refusing to see what is in front of me.

On the ground, folded neatly, are Nir's clothes.

The same clothes I saw him in on the beach. The same clothes the police found after he disappeared.

Red and blue striped Bermuda shorts. An "I heart NL" T-shirt.

On top of the folded shirt lies a folded yellow lined paper. No! *No!*

A sudden gust of wind blows from the shore and lifts the yellow paper. At first, just its edges ruffle lightly, but then the entire thing lifts in the air, tumbling over the folded clothes and onto the road.

In an instant, without any hesitation, the crab rushes on its tiny steps. It speeds around the clothes and chases the yellow paper. The wind seems to grow stronger, taking it further away from the crab. But the little critter is stubborn and resilient, and eventually it catches the paper in its claw. He then turns around and reverses its steps, coming in my direction. He stops right in front of me.

I know what it wants me to do. My heart tells me not to do it. I do it nevertheless.

I reach down and kneel on the ground. The little crab doesn't waiver. The yellow paper is folded in half. I touch it with the tip of my finger, afraid of its bite, the pain I know I will find inside. The crab let the paper go. Its swift movement unfolds the two halves of the paper without my permission. No! I don't want to see what's inside. I didn't ask for this!

I recognize the big round letters, Nir's handwriting. One line stubs straight into my heart.

I'm sorry. I can't do it anymore.

No!

No! I refuse to accept it!

The wind whistles around me. It picks up, swiping leaves and sand off the road. It snatches Nir's note from my grip. The paper floats in the air. I start running after it, trying to catch it. Sand enters my eyes, blurring my vision. I cannot give up. I must grab the note and destroy it. Make it change. Reverse whatever it means.

But the wind, it is so strong, as though the hand of God is pushing against me. I struggle with all my might. The yellow note with that awful line, only seven words but so much pain in them, leads me back to the beach. The water has changed. Monstrously sized waves rise and fall, crash into one another, and roll to the shore. I could not have survived my earlier jump into the water if it was as rough as it is now. I would have been swallowed whole, washed to the shore like Nir.

Nir. I see him standing on the beach with his back to me. He wears only a swimsuit and ignores the wind around him.

I run faster, down the street, down to the beach, down to where the water meets the sand. Down to my Nir.

Nir's sandcastle is in ruins. It is much larger now, taking an entire section of the beach. So many details are crushed—remnants of towers, a moat, bridges, two story buildings like the dorms in his *yeshiva*, a flat area that looks like a parking lot in front of a hospital. I do not have time to go around it. I must get to Nir as fast as I can to stop him from what he is about to do. I stomp through the mound, step on smashed hills and mountains, stumble in the depths of the moat, my hands flailing around me, destroying whatever is left to destroy.

Nir starts walking in the water. His feet are ankle high under the washing waves.

"Nir! Nir! Nirnir Nir Nirnir Nirrrrr!"

He does not turn around, does not waver. He continues his descent as if enchanted by the full moon.

I am too far to reach him, to hold him, to stop him.

He is now hip-deep in water. The high waves smash in front of him, splashes of white foamy water cover his shoulders and head.

"Nirrrr! Forgive me, Nir! Please, just stop!"

For a second, I think he stops. I think that he tilts his head, that he listens. I think he would now turn around. Come back to me.

He does not.

I am too late. I cannot save him.

CHAPTER 17

Wednesday, Fourth Day of the Shiva

TAMMY

"Ram, come quick," a shout came from the living room. "It's your dad! He collapsed again, hurry!"

Ram and Tammy jumped from the sofa bed and ran to the living room. A crowd of people blocked the way.

"Move away," Ram snapped at them while pushing his way through, Tammy right behind him. An ambulance siren blew in the distance, getting closer.

Good. Someone already called Magen David Adom, Tammy thought.

Ram reached the low sofa and kneeled down on the floor, holding his father's hand. Chaim lay on the sofa, white foam coming out the corner of his mouth, his eyes rolled up, and his entire body twitched.

"Is this what happened the other day?" Tammy asked urgently.

"No, nothing like that," Chava replied next to them. "On Monday he just fainted. Nothing like this! And he is a healthy man. It was poor Sarah who had health issues, God bless her dear soul." Her face was long and dark.

"We must get him to the hospital right now!" Ram said. "Something is very wrong."

Two paramedics came through the open front door. They were panting from the four-story run.

"Please, give us some space," one of them said while pulling a pair of latex gloves from one of the many pockets of his pants and putting them on. He was tall and skinny and didn't look ta day older than eighteen. The *kippah* on his head stated, "Don't Worry Be Happy," in a rainbow of colors. He calmly checked Chaim's pulse and cleared his airway.

"It looks like a stroke," he murmured to his partner, a dark-skinned man in his late thirties. The red star of David on the back of his vest stretched over his muscled body. "We will have to take him to the ER. Are you his daughter?" he asked Tammy.

"No." She pointed at Ram. "This is his son."

The paramedics continued their work. The younger one opened a sealed IV kit, stretched the clear plastic line, and prepared it quickly for administration. His hand movements were measured and efficient. His partner brought the stretcher they carried with them from the ambulance and arranged it parallel to the sofa.

"Hold this while we move him," the younger paramedic asked Tammy, handing her the IV bag. It was cold to the touch.

The younger paramedic held Chaim under his shoulder blades, supporting his head with his arms while his partner picked Chaim up by the legs. They moved Chaim as gently as possible to the stretcher; the younger confined Chaim's head to the stretcher while the older secured his torso and lower body.

It took them a long time to carry the stretcher down the stairs. The automatic lights in the staircase shut off every thirty seconds, and one of the neighbors turned it on again and again. The front doors of several apartments were ajar. Women stood on the landings, their eyes wide. At first, Tammy was astonished at what she interpreted as worry for Chaim's well-being. But the feeling quickly dissipated and changed to contempt, as what she saw in their eyes was curiosity.

A crowd gathered on the sidewalk. *Do they have to gawk like this? Why can't they just go on about their business and leave the poor man alone?* Tammy thought she recognized some of the faces from the *shiva* house, but most of them were strangers; onlookers who gathered around whenever an emergency service came along, wondering who is sick, what happened to him, feeding like vultures on other people's misfortunes. Even the traffic along the little street jammed, as each driver just *had* to look and see what was going on.

Ram paid no attention to the spectators. He jumped into the ambulance, crouching next to his dad. The older paramedic was already inside, tending to Chaim.

"Come." Ram held his hand out to help Tammy step into the clinical bowels of the vehicle. The younger paramedic pushed Tammy gently to the side as he slammed the two back doors shut. They barely missed Ram's outstretched hand.

"I'll see you at the hospital," Tammy shouted to Ram.

The young paramedic ran to the driver seat, and with no hesitation he started driving, breaking a way through the spectators. The sirens restarted their wail while he blasted his horn to underscore the urgency of his delivery.

Which hospital they are taking him to? Tammy couldn't remember hearing them saying. A gentle hand on her arm caught her attention. Chava was right next to her, still wearing her apron.

"Come with me," she said. "They are taking him to Tel Hashomer hospital. Let me first get my keys and we will be on our way." She ran back upstairs to fetch her purse, her swollen legs slowing her down.

"*Shir hamaalot mima'amakim keraticha Adonai.*" *From the depths, I have cried out to you, O Lord.* Millie stood on the sidewalk holding her prayer book close to her heart. Her eyes looked at the empty parking space that the ambulance occupied a moment ago. She continued her prayer silently, her mouth moving as she recited the *Tehillim* by heart. The people around them lingered.

Old women, dressed in long black skirts and gray sweaters that didn't leave much skin exposed, whispered to each other while pointing to Tammy and Millie. Behind them, at a comfortable distance, groups of men stood talking. Most of them were black-clad and bearded. On the other side of the road a group of small boys with long earlocks and big velvet *kippahs* played there with a ball, sweaty and passionate about their game, their shirts untucked, the strands of their *tzitzit* tassels hanging loose and long alongside their pants.

A sour smell of sweat and burned fuel filled the air. It stood still and thick around them.

"The car is around the corner." Chava emerged from the building, the car keys in her hand. She breathed heavily, and her face shone with perspiration, but she didn't slow down. She still wore her apron. "Come, Millie." She put an arm around the young girl and led her to the car. In her embrace, Millie looked younger and vulnerable. Tammy followed them into the car.

Chava maneuvered the traffic calmly, zigzagging at times between lanes, trying to avoid heavy traffic.

"So, you are more than just a friend from the army." It was not a question.

Tammy gazed quickly at Millie to see what her reaction would be. Millie had not stirred in the back seat, her head still buried in her prayer book. Tammy looked back at Chava and nodded.

"It's okay," Chava said. "You don't have to tell me more than you want; I can see for myself. I'm also not like my brother! He was nuts about that whole business with Nir and the woman. I told him it has gone too far, but he is stubborn. As cruel as it sounds, he is learning his lesson now."

Millie cried loudly from the back seat. Tammy turned around again, and this time Millie's face was buried in her hands, her entire body shaking. She was sobbing.

"It was my fault, it was all my fault," Millie was crying now uncontrollably.

Chava looked at her through the rearview mirror. "What are you talking about?" she asked, keeping careful eye on the road ahead.

"Let me," Tammy whispered to Chava. She turned farther to face Millie at the back sit. "Millie, look at me," she said sternly.

When Millie didn't raise her head, Tammy leaned over the back of her seat and reached for Millie's chin to raise her head up. Millie didn't resist, but her eyes were closed shut.

"Look at me," Tammy repeated.

This time Millie opened her eyes. They were bloodshot.

"It was not your fault what happened to your father." Millie shook her head violently. "It's also not your fault what happened to Nir," Tammy continued, sensing there was much more Millie blamed herself for. *The poor girl. What is she carrying on her shoulders?* "And it is not your fault about things that happened before that, or that your mother got sick and passed away."

At that, Millie wailed louder, throwing her head backward. At the same moment, the car came to a halt by the traffic ahead. Tammy quickly moved from the front seat to the back and put a gentle hand around Millie's shoulders.

"If I would have been a stronger believer…" Millie blurted between sobs, "… prayed harder… asked God to save them…"

"Darling Millie. Oh, darling Millie. You can't blame yourself for any of this. You were just a child. *Still* a child."

She felt how Millie melts into her embrace, sobbing. The poor girl needed a hug, needed someone to understand her. A mother.

They continued driving silently until they reached the hospital.

Tel Hashomer resembled a university campus more than a city hospital: Spread over a large area, vast green spaces and public plazas filled the land between buildings. Following the signs, Chava navigated through the winding roads until she found a parking lot close to the emergency room.

"Come with me. We will find out what is going on," she said and marched in ahead of them. A security guard stopped them.

"Your purse, please," he said in a thick Russian accent.

"My brother, he was just brought in—"

"I know. This is hospital, always people coming in. Now open bag."

Chava took the purse off her shoulder and unzipped it. "Even in a hospital!" she said, blowing air through her teeth.

"Especially in hospital," the guard said.

She looked at him while he checked her purse. "You are right. I am sorry, it's just that my—"

"I know, I know, your brother. Now go." He nodded toward the reception area.

"Thank you," Tammy said.

"*Refuah shlema*," he said to their backs. Speedy recovery.

At the broad semi-circular reception desk, a tired nurse looked at her computer monitor, searching for Chaim's name. Tammy couldn't stand the clutter around the nurse. Binders, printouts, stacks of folders, phones, and medical forms covered the desk. *How can they work in this mess?*

A set of sliding doors behind the desk buzzed, and Ram appeared from a long corridor. He was deep in thought and did not notice them. Tammy approached him, gently holding his hands in hers.

"Ram, sweetie. What is going on?"

He didn't reply. He just looked at her, his eyes glazed. He seemed to be in shock.

"Ram, where is your dad? What happened to him?" She kept her voice calm, but the way he looked frightened her.

"They are saying he had a stroke, but it's too early to know the damage," he said, gazing at a point in space ahead of him. "We should have brought him after he first collapsed! Why didn't I insist on taking him to the hospital then?" He slammed a palm onto his forehead, and heavy creases lined his brows. The pain in his eyes was raw.

"It's not your fault!" Tammy said. She looked into his eyes, and when she couldn't catch his attention, she stood directly in front of him and held both sides of his face in her hands. "It's not your fault, you hear me?"

Ram blinked. He finally saw her.

"You have done everything you could. He refused to go to the hospital. He is a grown man, responsible for his own decisions."

Ram blinked again. He finally nodded. His entire body slumped like a marionette on loose cords.

He let her lead him to a row of plastic chairs along the wall. Millie joined them and slumped into the seat on

Ram's other side. She cried silently, tears flowing down her cheeks. *This family has suffered so much,* Tammy thought. She hugged Ram, his body stiff in her embrace.

"They are taking him to the ICU." Chava came from the nurse who finally gave her some information. "I don't know when they will let us see him. We need to wait... I should call Asher Shalom, ask him to check with Rabbi Zechariah about the *shiva*... Get someone to send us some food..." She went back to the nurse and asked to use the phone.

Ram broke Tammy's embrace and stood up. He started pacing like a defendant waiting for his verdict.

***

Later, Asher Shalom arrived at the hospital with Rabbi Zechariah. By then they moved to the ICU's family waiting room. A large flat screen TV broadcasted the evening news. Although the volume was on mute, the pictures were graphic enough to unfold the evening's story. A subtitle declared: MOTHER DROWNED TWO CHILDREN IN BATHTUB.

What a shame, Tammy thought. *People here are fighting for their lives, and a crazy woman took her own kids' life. And where were her family and doctors? Couldn't they have treated her to prevent such a disaster?*

Millie sat nearby. Her focus was still into her prayer book. Tammy admired the way Millie channeled her fear and anxiety to something she believed would work to help her father—reciting chapter after chapter of *Tehillim*. *I wish it would be this easy in the secular world,* she sighed.

"How is your father doing?" Rabbi Zechariah asked Ram.

"I don't know. He had a stroke, and we can't see him yet."

Rabbi Zechariah sat down on one of the chairs. His eyes were kind and his voice soft. "We have to be strong for him, Ram. To pray to our Father in Heaven and ask for your father's full recovery. I will arrange for a few men to say *Tehillim*."

"Rabbi, what about the *shiva*?" Asher Shalom asked. "They have to complete sitting for the entire week. Ram and Millie..."

Ram looked at Asher Shalom angrily.

Rabbi Zechariah nodded. He stroked his beard slowly. After some thought, he said, "That's true. Unfortunately, Ram, this happened when you are obliged to sit *shiva* for your brother. You and Millie will have to go back home and complete it. Nothing we can do about your father. It's *Pikuach Nefesh*. His life is more valuable than performing any of the laws, so he must stay here. But your *mitzvah* right now is at home."

"*Go home?* Nir is dead, and nothing will bring him back, not even us sitting *shiva* for him or saying *Kaddish* hundred times a day! My father is still alive, and I need to be here for him when he wakes up."

Rabbi Zechariah's gaze softened. "I understand—" he started.

"He must go," Asher Shalom said. "That's the *halacha*, and he must do it."

Rabbi Zechariah looked at Asher Shalom. Then he turned back to Ram. "I understand how you feel Ram. I pray to God that Chaim will heal. I think he would want you to complete the *shiva*. Not just for the dead's sake and for his *neshamah*, but also for yours. For Millie. You need that time to heal."

"What we need is to stay here and see that our father is okay!" He turned to Tammy. "Can you believe this? I *need* to go back to the *shiva*. It's the *mitzvah*," he spat the last word, "more than making sure my dad is okay!"

"Do it," Tammy said. "Go. I will stay here. Take Millie with you."

Ram looked like she struck him in the face.

At that, Millie stopped her quiet chanting. Until that moment she seemed detached from the conversation around her. "I'm not going anywhere," she said.

"You will not do good to anyone waiting here," Tammy addressed both Ram and Millie. "In any case, you can't see him yet. Just go, and I'll be fine. I'll call you the minute he wakes up."

Ram's defiance broke down as quickly as it started. He looked tired and defeated. "Are you sure?"

Millie, on the other hand, shook her head and straightened herself in her chair, as if rooting in deeper so that no one could move her away.

The waiting room's door opened, and a racket of voices came in as a group of men entered—Meir Ben-Israel and his followers; the entire entourage.

"Ram! How is your father the *tzadik* doing?" Ben-Israel asked loudly from the other side of the large room.

"What are you doing here?" Ram asked coldly when Ben-Israel reached him.

"The minute we heard Reb Levi fell ill we all drove here. Don't worry, we are going to have a vigil, say *Tehillim*, and pray for his full recovery. You will see, it will be a miracle!"

His followers nodded their heads in unison, echoing back, "A miracle!" Forming a large circle, some of them took out prayer books. They were ready to start their routine.

Asher Shalom seemed unsure what to do. He rocked from foot to foot, trying to decide whether he wanted to join Ben-Israel's vigil or stay with his family members. Rabbi Zechariah put a hand on his shoulder, keeping him in place.

When Asher Shalom looked at his rabbi with question in his eyes, Rabbi Zechariah nodded slightly. Without a word, Asher Shalom stopped his fidgeting. Defeated somehow, he stepped behind Rabbi Zechariah.

"We should go, Ram," Rabbi Zechariah said calmly.

This finally convinced Ram. "I am out of here," he said to Tammy. "Millie, you are coming with me. Tammy, are you sure you can handle these guys?"

"Of course," Tammy said. "They are harmless. Not as tough as my soldiers..." She winked.

Ram smiled at that. The first smile she has seen on his face for so long.

"I am staying here," Millie said.

"With these lunatics?" Ram's voice rose.

Millie ignored him, stubborn in her resolve to stay close to her father.

Rabbi Zechariah approached Ram from behind. "Ram, please let me," he said softly.

Ram moved aside, sighing heavily. He decided to extend his attention to the newcomers.

"Okay, Ben-Israel, listen to me. You are in no way allowed to bother my father. Do you understand?" Ben-Israel had his attention now. "I am going to give direct orders to the nurses and doctors not to allow you or any of your friends into the corridor over there or wherever my father is. Even if he is awake and asking for you, you should decline and stay here. Understood?"

"*Tzadik ben tzadik!*" Ben-Israel opened his arms wide. "You *are* your father's son. Making sure nothing disturbs him. This is *kibud horim*! I admire you for that! Don't worry. I'll not go close to him, not until you come back and give me your blessing."

"Good!" Ram said. He took Tammy to the side. "I don't trust him," he whispered to her. "Call me if this nut case is doing anything strange or going into the ICU! And if my father wakes up…"

"Of course, Ram. Don't worry."

"I will check in later on."

He looked at her a minute longer.

Asher Shalom, Chava, and Rabbi Zechariah were waiting for him. Millie joined from behind. Whatever Rabbi Zechariah told her had convinced her to return home. Tammy followed their backs, shrinking in the distance, until they were all swallowed in the elevator. Of all of them, at that moment Tammy's heart ached for Millie.

CHAPTER 18

CHAIM

I cannot do anything.

I am frozen. My legs are as heavy as lead. I am rooted on the beach. My hands stretch out reaching for Nir. They get nowhere. My mouth is parched. I feel the salty air and sprays of water on my face, in my eyes, up my nostrils. I can do nothing to stop him, to save him.

Nir didn't die swimming. He killed himself.

He killed himself, and it was my fault. My fault. *My fault!* I killed him.

I see him no more.

The water swallows him, tosses him upside down, pulls him to its depth, leaving me with nothing.

I cannot see any of it.

I can see it all.

His young body jerks. His head spins forcefully from side to side. Bubbles come out of his mouth, his eyes are wide open, the saltwater stinging into them. His hair floats around his face, back and forth, adopting the rhythm of the waves.

I can see it all.

His lungs burn, bursting with water. His eyes bulge in their sockets, searching around helplessly, looking for something to hold onto. His legs kick and push, sending him deeper into the abyss.

I can see it all.

His hands clutch his neck and his fingers dig deep into his skin, denting his lean muscles. His tongue flies out of his mouth as more water invades him.

I can see it all.

His entire body jerks in one last effort. Then relaxes, giving up. His hands lose their grip, and his arms float to his sides. His body arches, stretches, and floats in mid-water. His hair sweeps his face gently. His eyelids relax, closing slowly to half gaze. His eyeballs settle back halfway into the skull.

I can see it all.

And then, I can see nothing.

***

The sea calms down. It fed on its latest victim, relaxing now after a violent meal. The waves cease, and the surface of the water flattens uninterrupted. It is quiet. Dead quiet.

I fall to my knees.

I cry.

What have I done?

I cry more, lying on the sand. Rivers of tears flow from my eyes in all directions. I have never cried this way, not when my parents died, not when Sarah passed away.

Time is meaningless in this place. Sunrise evaporates the darkness, and nightfall swallows the daylight. For how long, how many times, I can't tell.

Suddenly I hear a voice calling my name.

"Chaim."

A woman's voice.

"Chaim."

It is familiar, but in my grief, I do not place it right away.

"Chaim, I am right here."

The voice calls me to come to her.

"Chaim."

I do not want to move. All I wish is to stay where I am, to disappear. But the voice does not relent.

"Chaim, come here."

I try to clear my head, to focus. Whose voice is it? Calling me here? I sit up, and with my free hand I clear the sand from my face and wipe my eyes. My other hand, the one holding the little stone, is stiff in its clench. I try to move my fingers, wiggle them slightly to release the tension. But they refuse to abide, as if my fist fused to become part of that rock and the rock part of me.

"Chaim."

Here it is again. Sarah! It is Sarah's voice. I should have recognized it immediately. I am in worse shape than I imagined.

"Chaim, right here. Come to me."

I stand up, reflexively wiping more sand off my shirt and pants, ignoring the stiffness and pain in my clenched hand. Nothing seems important right now. I hear Sarah, and I should find her, and I should stay with her, beg her to keep me right here, with her. I start walking toward the buildings, but then I stop, hesitating, not sure this is where she called me from.

"Chaim."

Her voice sounds far away. I am going the wrong way. I turn around and look on either side of the shore. Voices are carried farther over water, and she is nowhere to be seen. I must choose one direction and start that way.

"Chaim, what is taking you so long?"

I am on the right track. Her voice is stronger now. I move faster, running on the sandy beach.

"I am coming. Where are you? Can you show yourself?" I shout and squint to see better.

"Chaim, I am right here. Can't you see me?"

This time, her voice is farther. What happened? Am I going the wrong way? I turn around again and run in the other direction.

"Chaim, I don't have much time. Hurry."

I must hurry though I cannot see her. I run, panting, the sand making it harder to move fast.

"Chaim, right here."

Her voice comes from behind me. I turn, and she is right there.

"You found me!" She smiles.

"Sarah, my Sarah." She is amazingly beautiful, young and vibrant. She looks just like she did after giving birth to Nir, twenty-one years ago. Her face is smooth and glowing. Her hair tied tightly in a bun, a few strands falling out in the front. She tucks them behind her ear. She does not wear makeup. My most gorgeous Sarah.

"Chaim, my darling," she says. "You have been through enough pain. You deserve to rest now. To live your life."

I cannot say a word. My throat is tight, and I swallow hard. I try to speak nevertheless. "Nir—" I burst into a new crying fit. "He—Sarah, it is terrible."

"I know, my darling. I know," she says.

"What can I do?" I ask.

"There is nothing you can do now. What's done is done."

"So why am I here? I must do something, save him somehow."

"You know it is not possible, Chaim. My dear, poor Chaim." She pauses. Then she says, "There are Ram and Millie. Be good to them."

"I cannot go back! I need to stay here, with you."

She looks at me, her eyes dark and sad.

"I cannot go back! How will I face everyone? I killed him… It was all because of me!"

"My poor, poor Chaim," Sarah says. She raises her hand to me, but as she does, I know she cannot touch me, and I cannot touch her. Just like everyone else I have seen before. But she *does* see me, and she *does* talk to me. A sweet scent fills my nostrils—her smell. I realize how much I missed it.

"You cannot stay here, Chaim," she says. "I cannot stay here, either. I must go back."

"So take me with you!" I say.

She shakes her head fiercely. "No! You must go back home and take care of Ram and Millie."

In my grief, I forgot about the rest of my life. In the hours or days that I followed Nir, and cried for him, for myself, I forgot that I still have Ram and Millie. Sarah is right. They need me.

"I will go back," I finally say. "But please, tell me what I can do to ease the pain. How can I repent?"

A flicker crosses over her smooth face, like she is fading in and out of existence. In that instant I sense that there is something I can do, something she doesn't tell me.

"Sarah, I beg you, if there is something I can do to make things right, please tell me. I will do anything!"

She looks at me sternly. Then, resolved, she says, "My darling, take care of yourself."

I want her to say more, but she turns around and starts to walk away from me.

"Sarah," I call her. "Wait, Sarah…"

She turns around to look at me. She waits.

"I miss you… I—I love you."

She smiles. "Me too, my darling. Me too."

She starts turning around. I see her hesitate. She stops and looks at me again. She had changed her mind.

Then, she tells me what I should do.

And while she talks and my attention is completely on her moving lips and beautiful eyes, her hands gently touch mine, holding in their warmth the fist that wraps over Nir's little stone. I pay no attention to the warmth emanating from her, not until she finishes talking and looks down toward our hands. Only then I see her hands are glowing, holding my open palm in them, and the little stone is gone.

CHAPTER 19

Wednesday to Saturday, Fourth to Seventh Days of the Shiva

RAM

It was a sleepless night for Ram. Too many thoughts ran through his head. He tried to distract himself by researching online for stroke prognosis. He wanted to be ready and knowledgeable when he spoke with Chaim's doctor in the morning. The forecast was not good.

> **TAMMY:** Are you awake?

The little cell phone buzzed next to his laptop, the vibrations amplified on the hard surface table and the dead quiet of the house. Tammy wasn't sleeping either. He picked it up and texted back.

> **RAM:** I can't sleep... online, reading about stroke :(
> **TAMMY:** I'm so sorry Ram.
> **RAM:** Where are you? I wish you could be here
> **TAMMY:** Tel Hashomer
> **RAM:** Oh god, are you still at the hospital?
> **TAMMY:** Yes. Chava is here too. I told her she can go home and I'll stay, but she insists that I should go instead

A few seconds passed. Then,

TAMMY: He is still unconscious. The doctor doesn't tell us much

Ram typed something in reply. The words morphed into a blur, floating in front of his eyes in the middle of the little lit screen. He shook his head and squeezed his eyes hard. When he opened them again and his vision focused enough to read, nothing made much sense. He quickly searched for the phone screen and speed-dialed Tammy's number.

"Hey, honey," she answered before the first ring. Her whisper was soothing in his ear.

"Tammy…" He broke. Tears pushed at the back of his eyes, the pressure so intense he doubled over and rolled down from his chair to the bed beside the desk. Even in this moment of extreme sorrow, he tried to muffle his cries, burrowing his head into the pillow.

"Ram, oy Ram. Listen, I am coming over."

"No! It's the middle of the night…"

"Don't be silly! I'll take a taxi from the hospital and will be there right away. Don't hang up!"

He didn't open his eyes until she arrived. Her soft breathing on the other end of the line calmed him down. Chava fell asleep on a chair in the waiting room, so Tammy left a note for her at the nurses' station, speaking in a soft voice as she wrote it down. He listened to her voice when she gave the address to the taxi driver and then thanked him for the ride. He regained some strength to pick himself up off the bed and open the door for her when she arrived.

The house was quiet. The only lights came through the cracks in the shutters from a street light outside. Tammy smiled in the dark when he reached his hand to hold hers and led her to his room.

They didn't speak. They laid on the narrow bed. Tammy held him in her arms, his head on the small of her shoulder where he could hear her heartbeat. She must have felt his unruly facial hair against her thin shirt. Her body heat spilled into him through her fingertips, her palms, the pale, smooth inner arms, her neck, even her hips and stomach through the fabric of her clothes, slowly, until their warmth merged into one.

Tammy caressed his short hair as he spoke. "From what I read, brain damage is irreversible. There might be some physiotherapy techniques that can bring some lost functions. They say people can live for years after suffering a stroke, but the chances for another one are much higher. Any permanent loss of control over parts of his body would most likely require constant care, a companion to help him with simple daily routines; feeding, changing, showering, going to the bathroom."

"Don't run into any conclusions from Googling," Tammy said. "Talk tomorrow with Chaim's doctors. We will be much smarter."

Ram didn't say more.

They lay side by side until dawn. Tammy dozed for the remaining of the night, but Ram was unable to sleep.

***

The next day, the minute they heard from the hospital their father was awake, Ram and Millie rushed to see him, despite Rabbi Zechariah's insistence on staying at home for the *shiva*. How could they have stayed away?

"Abba, God willing, you will be fine. You will see," Millie was first to speak. Their father's hospital room was well lit, though not from the sun shining outside. It was a bright day for the rest of the world, but for Ram and Millie, seeing their father in his new state, it felt dim and cloudy.

Chaim's doctor kept him sedated for the remainder of the night, trying to reduce any additional pressure on his brain. He suffered a medium sized Ischemic stroke, which affected the left side of his body. His eye and mouth droop slightly and his left arm dangled heavily by his body.

"The doctors are optimistic," Millie continued, "and so am I. God *will* cure you. I know it." Her face was white and her eyes wide, but her voice was steady and confident. She clutched her *siddur*, its cover moist from the sweat on her palms.

Dear Millie. Her faith is so strong, Ram admired her silently. She probably recited *Tehillim* all night.

As Millie tried to encourage her father in the only way she knew, Chaim tried to smile. It looked like a sideway question mark. His good eye closed; he was tired.

"Abba, are you okay? Do you want us to go so you can rest?"

Chaim shook his head slowly. "Nah," he said with effort. "Sta... Si..."

Millie looked at Ram. He nodded, pointing to the chair next to the bed. "Millie, sit here. I'll grab another chair from next door."

He left the room, disturbed. As he came out, Ben-Israel greeted him outside. He was leaning on the wall, waiting. A few of his friends hovered behind.

"How is he?" He jumped from his position at the wall.

Ram sighed. *I don't have patience for this.* To Ben-Israel, he said, "He is exhausted. There is some damage to the left side of his body; it's paralyzed."

"Is he out of immediate danger?"

"Yes, I think he is."

"*Ha'shevach La'El.*" Praised The Lord. Ben-Israel clasped his hands, kissed the tip of his fingers, then stretched his arms skyward, and looking up he cried, "Thank you, Abba!"

The Ben-Israelites were as equally excited upon hearing the news. They clapped each other on the back, all smiles, a few of them repeating their leader's mime and exclaims of gratitude to their God.

"When can we see him? We want to praise God together with him!"

Not again, Ram thought. To Ben-Israel, he said, "It's not a good idea, he is frail and upset—"

"We will cheer him up!" Ben-Israel said and started humming a tune. He clapped his hands for rhythm.

"Please," Ram said, "calm down, I will tell him you are here and asking for his well-being. That's it!"

"Okay, *tzadik ben tzadik.* We'll stay right here!" And he joined his friends, singing quietly in the background.

Ram couldn't stop a small smile. You could say a lot of things about Ben-Israel, but his optimism was catching.

He found a chair at the nurses' station and brought it to his father's room.

"Ben-Israel and his minions are asking about you," he told Chaim.

"Tell them to go away!" Chaim blurted. With half of his mouth paralyzed it sounded like, "Ell em ta g' wae."

"Abba, don't get worked up. I told them already they can't come in here. These guys are unbelievable. They started singing and dancing when they heard you woke up."

"Ah 'ont wa t'see em!"

"Abba, please, calm down," Millie said, looking at Ram pleadingly. "He can't get upset like that…"

"Don't worry, Abba. Forget about them. They won't get anywhere in here. You can rest now."

Ram's words did nothing to calm Chaim down. He closed his eyes wearily, and his breathing labored. When he opened them, he looked at Ram and said slowly, trying to make each word count and understood, "Ell… em… to … go… awa… no… ehaye… eti… hee! No. Ehaye eti…. No ehaye eti…" He trailed off, exhausted.

Millie looked at him, then at Ram, and back at her father. "What is he saying? I can't understand him." Tears welled in her eyes.

Ram only nodded, his gaze fixed on his father. He understood. *No Mechaye Metim. No resurrector.* Finally, his father came through.

"Okay, Abba, I will tell them and ask them to leave. Please calm down. You must calm down."

His father was crying now, his body shaking violently. A nurse ran into the room, alerted by his monitor.

"What is happening?" Millie cried.

"You have to leave now," the nurse said.

"Abba!"

Ram held her shoulders. He worried about her. *Would I have to be her father now too?* But first things first. He had to make an end to the harassment outside. Blood rushed into his head as he barged out of the room.

When he saw Ben-Israel outside, Ram leaped at him. He held Ben-Israel by his shirt lapels and pushed him hard into the wall. His face was inches away.

"Go away and stop disturbing us!" he shouted at Ben-Israel. "My dad doesn't want you or your bandits here!"

Ben-Israel squirmed under his hold. "*Tzadik—*" he started.

"Stop calling me *Tzadik*! I am not a *tzadik,* and my father is not a *tzadik.* Just do as you are told and leave us alone!"

"But, the *Mechaye*! He came to your dad! He believes in him!"

"Bullshit! He doesn't believe in this... this idol worship! He just told me there is no *Mechaye Metim*! There is no *Mekubal*! No Eliyahu Hanavi!"

Millie stood by, a terrified look on her face.

"No... *No*! I don't believe you!" Ben-Israel retorted. "You never believed, and you always disliked us. You didn't see Nir on your own. You are envious of your father—"

"Are you crazy?" Ram couldn't believe his ears. "Do you even hear yourself?"

He pushed Ben-Israel harder, crashing his back to the wall. Then he dropped his hold and went to the nurses' station, approaching the first nurse he saw.

"Call security for me, or the police! I want these men out of here!"

"Sir, please calm down," the nurse said, "if you can tell me what the issue is, I will see how I can help you."

"This man, the one that looks like he lives on the hills—" He pointed at Ben-Israel.

Ben-Israel started to leave and indicated to his friends to follow him. "We will pray for your father, the *tzadik,*" he said. "And for you, *tzadik ben tzadik.* And your brother's spirit."

"Never mind," Ram said to the nurse. "We have to leave now. My dad needs to rest. Can you please call us when we can see him again?" He didn't wait for her reply. "And if this guy or any of his friends come back, I want you to call me immediately. Okay?"

The nurse didn't like his tone, but she disliked, even more, her patients being disturbed. She nodded. "I will."

Ram left her his cell phone number.

***

The *shiva* ended uneventfully. *Shabbat* was the seventh and last day, and as it is forbidden to mourn on the holy day, the last services in the house were held on Friday.

Ben-Israel didn't show up again. During the morning service Ram spotted one of his followers, Gilad. He sat on the sideline of the small *minyan* of praying men, looking around in all directions. He was looking for Chaim, and when it was obvious that Chaim would not join them, he quickly folded his *tallit* and *tefillin* and hurried out.

Good riddance! Ram hoped he would never see Gilad, Ben-Israel, or any of their friends.

"I don't think we will hear from them again."

Ram turned around. Chaim's friend, Baruch Langer, stood there, his gaze still on the open door from which Gilad just left.

"I sure hope so," Ram said.

"I have heard they found their next victim," Baruch whispered.

"Next victim?"

"Another sighting, another *shiva* house. This one in kibbutz Yotvata, of all places!" He started laughing, a deep throaty rolling laughter. "Just imagine," he blurted between outbursts, "maybe, this time, their *Mekubal* is a Bedouin on a camel... ha ha ha... Or maybe... maybe the *kibbutznik* from the cowshed who milks the cows! Ha ha ha..."

Ram could not hold his calm any longer, and he broke into a hearty laughing spell. When he and Baruch saw the other men in the room turn to them, raising their eyebrows in unison, their laughter did what it usually does in these situations—it grew stronger.

No Ben-Israelite showed up after that.

***

Shabbat gave Ram and Millie a needed break. They spent it with their father, from sundown on Friday evening 'til darkness the following night. Tammy offered to stay with them. Ram insisted she should go back home. She missed too many days at the base, and there was nothing much she could do to help his father.

"We will be right here, and as much as I hate spending *Shabbat* at the hospital, I need a break from the house, the constant attention of people hovering around, the craziness of the last few days," Ram told her. "I just need some quiet, some time to think."

Her eyes were warm and accepting. The long embrace she gave him before departing reassured him that she was okay with his reasons. He loved her for that.

Chaim slept most of the time, and either Ram or Millie was always at his bedside. They did not exchange many words. The beeps and clicks of the medical instruments, accompanied by the low hum of the hospital's air conditioning, kept them company. It was interrupted only by the busy, yet short, businesslike chatter of the visiting doctors and nurses.

Ram and Millie returned home on Saturday night after three stars shone in the dark sky, and *Shabbat* was over.

The *shiva* was over too.

CHAPTER 20

After the Shiva

RAM

After the *shiva*, Millie returned to the *ulpana* high school she attended. She wanted to stay home with Ram and help him deal with their father's condition. Ram convinced her to go back to her routine, to see her friends and teachers, study for tests and keep busy. This would be the only way for her to be distracted, to move on with life.

"You will come home every other weekend, and we can talk on the phone every day," he told her. "You must not neglect your studies… That's what Abba and Imma would have liked you to do." And that was the line he knew would convince her in the end. He saw the resolve in her eyes and her beloved *Tehillim* in her hands. *She will be all right*, he hoped.

Ram considered his father's future. Who would take care of him once he was released from the hospital? He did not know the extent of his dad's needs, but he knew it would be impossible for him to handle while his job was far away up north.

The options were limited. Sponsoring and employing a foreign worker caretaker would be complicated and costly. He could ask his aunt Chava to help, but how much time would she be able to spare between her family and work? He could hire an Israeli nurse for several hours every day. But what would happen the rest of the time?

The head nurse of his father's physician explained the physical and emotional care involved. "The best thing for your father's recovery," she concluded, "is to be with someone he loves."

That left only himself.

After a week in the hospital, Chaim was released. His doctor referred him to a physical therapy program. He was to come three times a week to the outpatient department and work with a therapist for a couple of hours each time. That would be manageable. Ram scheduled a handicap accessible taxi to pick him up from home, drop him off at the hospital, and then collect him again after the appointment. The rest of the time would be more complicated to arrange.

In the end, Ram took a few months off without pay from the army. He moved to his father's apartment, to his old room. Chaim was happy to have him there. He insisted on paying Ram an allowance. Better than bringing a stranger to his home, he said. Besides, the disability insurance he received would cover some of the expenses.

The first *Shabbat* after coming from the hospital, Chaim insisted on going to the morning prayers. Ram borrowed a wheelchair from *Ezer MeTzion*, a medical equipment charity. Millie was home from the *ulpana*. Food was stacked in the fridge, courtesy of Chaim's friends, mainly the ladies in the group. They even provided home-baked *challah* bread and rolls. They were still piping hot when one of the husbands made the delivery.

Tammy came on Friday and helped Ram to clean the house and tidy it up, throw some dirty laundry in the machine, and shop for some necessities. Ram missed not seeing her every day. He hoped this would be a short-term solution.

When Chaim saw Tammy, he smiled his new crooked smile.

"*Shalom*, Chaim. I'm happy to see you again outside of the hospital," she said.

"Ee too!" he said. His voice was still slurry, but he was not deterred. "Ca you 'elieve—" he panted, "is is how a' loo now? Hal' up an' hal' dow?" He emphasized it with a broader smile, raising his good hand up in the air.

"I see you didn't lose your sense of humor. That's good!"

"You brough' it ba' whe' you came 'rough the doo'."

Tammy laughed. "Chaim, don't tease me..."

They were giggling when Ram entered the room. "What's so funny?" he asked, puzzled.

"Nothin'," Chaim said sheepishly.

Tammy mouthed, *He is all right!*

Ram convinced Tammy to stay with them 'til Sunday. She planned to sleep over with one of her friends in Tel Aviv.

"Won't it bother your father if I stay to sleep here?"

"Don't worry. This is for me to deal with. I will set up a bed for you with Millie or give you my room and I'll sleep on the sofa."

"No, not *that* sofa! You had enough of it during the *shiva*," she said. "I'll be okay with Millie."

"I'm sorry, you know we can't... not here..."

"It's okay, honey. I know. Don't worry about it. It might give Millie and me some time to talk, for her to know me better..."

"Good. So it's settled."

***

After a week, they developed a daily routine. Ram woke Chaim up early in the morning and helped him shower and dress. They took the long trek down the stairs to Chaim's car, parked under the building. Ram drove them to the synagogue for the morning service. He helped Chaim to put on his prayer shawl and *tefillin*, then held the prayer book for him as they followed the service. On days that Chaim had physical therapy, they ate breakfast at the hospital's cafeteria, killing some time before the appointment. On other days they returned home, where his dad sat most of the day watching TV. The hardest part was returning upstairs. Ram considered moving to a building with an elevator. The physical therapist said it was a blessing in disguise. As tedious and time-consuming, going up and down the stairs forced Chaim to exercise.

Chaim's friends visited quite often. His chess club associates came to play his beloved game, but Chaim was too frustrated when he could not focus for as long as he used to. Several of their lady friends baked for them, stocking their refrigerator and freezer.

After lunches, Chaim sat on the brown sofa with the daily *Yediot Aharonot* newspaper, which came in the mail. Ram tried to convince him to switch to digital, for reading up to the minute news. He always said he's old-fashioned—he liked the feel of the paper in his hands, unfolding the news section by section, getting his fingertips blackened with ink. Ram noticed, though, that his reading habits did change. Where in the past the obituaries section was ignored, now it was the first section his father checked. Every day Ram fetched the paper from the mailbox at the lobby of the building and brought it upstairs for Chaim. And every day, Chaim opened it gingerly, looked for the latest death announcements, reading them carefully, as if he had lost something important and they were the key to locating whatever it was.

Once done, he put it aside carefully, a look of disappointment on his face. He did not say anything, and Ram did not ask. He usually continued with the rest of the paper, and when done, opened the obituaries again, scanning it a second time.

On the weekends, Millie would come home from the *ulpana*. The head principal gave her a special permission to spend every *Shabbat* with her family, rather than every other week. She helped as much as she could, though at times Ram made her take a break and study for a test or spend an hour with a friend.

On some weekends Tammy joined them as well. Over time, Ram noticed how her visits positively affected Chaim. When he saw her entering the apartment, his father would straighten up in his chair, run his good hand in his hair to put it in place, and fix the *kippah* on his head. He would greet her with a smile and would be relaxed in her company.

"She is a catch!" he told Ram one *Shabbat* afternoon when Ram helped him change and get ready for his afternoon nap. Ram was bending in front of Chaim, unbuttoning his father's white dress shirt while Chaim sat on the edge of his bed.

"Eh... if you say so," was all Ram could manage. He stole a glance at Chaim to see how serious he was, and saw no humor there, then continued with the next button.

"Yes, yes, I can see your mother in her. She is kind and good spirited."

"She is very different from Imma." Ram pulled on Chaim's right-hand sleeve, loosening the shirt on that end 'til it hung crumpled behind Chaim's back, then walked around to pull the other sleeve away.

"All that matters is that you fit together. And I believe she will be a good mother."

Ram held the shirt up like a flimsy shield between him and his father. "Hmmm. You know, Abba, she grew in a *Hashomer Hatzair* kibbutz, right?"

"Yeah, yeah," Chaim nodded.

"… And she doesn't have a religious background…"

"You think I'm stupid? I know that."

"… And she was—well, she *is*—in the army. Not a soldier-teacher or national service like the religious girls, but a regular soldier—"

"Yeah, I know, I know. So what's your point?" Chaim's voice was raspy.

"—and it doesn't bother you?"

"What doesn't bother me?"

"That she is not religious? That she is my girlfriend?"

Chaim looked at him gravely. Then he burst out laughing. His shoulders, previously wide and proud, were now fallen and hunched. They heaved and shook with effort as the laughter came out of him in forced spurts.

"What's so funny?" Ram asked.

"You; your face; how serious you are," Chaim chuckled, then his outburst changed to a fit of coughs. Ram realized he was still holding the white shirt in his hands. He dropped it on a chair nearby, and picked up a half filled glass of water from the side table. He handed it to Chaim.

"Listen, Ram," Chaim finally said. His eyes had a fixed resolute in them, the previous waves of laughter and coughs forgotten. "You may not see deep inside me, but I have seen more than you think I have."

He took brief breaks as he talked. Talking for long was still taxiing and he would get exhausted. Ram listen patiently. Chaim's face strained. It was important for him to find the right words.

"I know now who you are and who you are not," he continued. "And you are not the little boy you used to be, nor the grown-up man your mother *zichronah livracha* and I thought we would raise. We had dreams, and that's what they were: just dreams. No one is exactly what others expect them to be. It's as simple as that.

"I know you are not who you show yourself to me. I'm not blind. I have seen how the prayers stopped interesting you and how you would not practice many of the *mitzvot* like when you were younger. I saw you one time walking to the bus station without your *kippah*. So I knew having a girlfriend would be just natural. And I'm sure you do more than just hold hands, right?"

He did not wait for an answer.

"I already lost your mom and your brother." His voice choked. Tears appeared at the corner of his eyes. Ram handed him a Kleenex. He dabbed his eyes with it and tried with difficulty to blow his nose.

"I am not planning to lose any more time or loved ones!" Chaim's voice raised. His back straightened and his shoulders widened.

Ram was lost for words. For a second there, he saw his father as he was years ago, young and tall and powerful. And for the first time, he saw his father exposed. Here in front of him was a man who lost so much, his spirit and body broken, and finally he said those words. *Loved ones. Love.*

Finally, he found his strength, and the words came out. "I am happy about that, Abba," he said gently. "Now get some rest. You need it if you want to have more time with us."

His father didn't resist. Ram kneeled down and removed his slippers. And then, quietly, without any word, Chaim lay down in bed, thin and pale. He closed his eyes.

Ram covered him with the duvet, then turned around and went to the door.

"I love you, Ram…"

He turned to look at Chaim. His eyes were closed. He was asleep.

"I love you too, Abba."

He could not remember when was the last time that they exchanged these words.

CHAPTER 21

Three Months After the Shiva

CHAIM

"Ram, I need you to drive me to Herzliya today."

Ram and I are finishing our lunch, a simple meal of baked chicken and potatoes with Arabic salad on the side. It is quiet at lunch, but we both don't mind it. We have become used to each other's company, and lengthy talking feels like a chore these days.

"Herzliya? Who do you need to see there?"

"Nobody important. I just need you to take me. It won't take long."

"Okay… Do you have the address?"

"Yes."

"When do you need to be there?"

"Around six tonight should be fine."

Ram nods his head. A look of confusion is in his eyes, but he doesn't push further for more information. I am thankful for that.

"Now help me. I need my nap."

***

Around four in the afternoon, I lock myself in the bathroom. Using my electric razor, I shave thoroughly. It is hard to see around the corners of my newish face, but I do my best.

During my recovery, Ram helps me with this task. I do not bother shaving daily, letting my facial hair grow for two or three days. Today is the first time since returning from the hospital that I shave on my own, and I want to have enough time to do so, given how slow I am. Once I am done, I shower and dress. When I exit the bathroom, Ram looks up from his book and smiles.

"Nice job!" He looks satisfied.

At quarter past five we are downstairs, sitting in my car, Ram at the steering wheel. I hope I can drive again one day. Immobility is one of the hardest aspects of my disability. It saddens me for a moment, then I remember where we are going, and I do my best to ignore the inconvenience.

"Okay, I'm ready. Where are we going?" Ram asks.

I take a folded piece of paper from my shirt's pocket. It is a page from the newspaper, which I unfold carefully, pinning it down with my bad hand and smoothing it on my knee with the good one. Today's date is printed at the top of the page. I point to a black frame nestled amongst other similar ones, second column from the right.

"Here is the address."

Ram looks at the paper, then at me. "Are you serious? You want to go to a *shiva* house?"

"Yes. That's where I need to go."

"Tzvia Shmueli," Ram reads. "Did you know her? Who is she?"

"Just go," I say, my gaze on the road ahead. *Please don't argue,* I beg him without uttering the words. *I won't be able to explain.*

"Okay, if that's what you want." He had heard my unspoken request. His voice, on the other hand, reveals his curiosity, and yes, also resentment. I should have explained more, but that will come in time. Right now, I need to heal and do some good to others.

We drive silently. Although it is rush hour, traffic is light. Thank God for small favors. This is good; Ram wouldn't get upset navigating the busy streets.

After asking for directions a couple of times, Ram finally finds the address. He parks the car nearby, at the curb of the quiet road. Usually, a parking spot on a street with a *shiva* house is hard to come by, so Ram looks happy to find a close spot. The house I am heading to—a private residence in a neighborhood of detached single homes hidden behind tall walls—has a hip-high stone fence topped with a live hedge. It is green and lavish, dotted with red hibiscus buds. An obituary sign is attached to the wrought iron gate.

TZVIA SHMUELI Z"L

Under the big letters of her name, the time of the funeral—which was the previous day—and the family sitting *shiva*: three daughters, Leah, Tamar, and Yael. The grieving family includes grandkids and great grandkids.

The gate is open, and other people come through and walk to the house.

"Are you sure you want to go inside?" Ram asks. "Did you know this woman?"

"No, I didn't know her. And yes, I'm sure I want to go inside. You can wait for me in the car."

"But—" he hesitates. "I don't understand why we are here!"

"I will tell you one day, I promise. Right now, please, just let me go in."

"Is it related to Nir and how you saw him during the *shiva*?"

I look at him for a long time, but I will not say, not yet. There will be time for that. Finally, I open the car door and push myself outside. It is an awkward maneuver with my bad leg and weak hand, but if I need to, I will go on my own.

"Okay, okay!" Ram exclaims, "I'll come with you."

"That's fine, you can come or stay. Just don't be in the way."

We step slowly up the stone lane leading to the main entrance. The house is lit, and we hear voices of people talking inside. We enter the house from a wide veranda with French doors stacked open all the way. It is a nice evening, already warm for the season, and the light breeze circulates the air from the front yard and into the spacious living room.

Once inside, I can tell immediately that the owners are not religious people by the way the women dress and the type of *kippahs* the men wear. Some men and all the kids have no *kippahs* on their heads. One can tell by the absence of religious books on the bookshelves, and by the scarcity of Judaica items on the shelves. One can tell by the way the men and women interact, how they kiss each other on the cheeks, how they give comforting hugs. And, one can tell by the flowers they bring to *shiva* houses.

"So, what are we doing here?" Ram whispers.

"A *mitzvah*."

***

I walk slowly; my bad leg is holding me back. Damn thing! There is time. I don't need to hurry anywhere. Still, I have a mission to fulfill.

I find the mourners' seats, three low plastic recliner chairs. In them sit three middle-aged women. They look alike, although each has her unique features. One, probably

Leah, the oldest, is around my age, if I had to guess. She dyes her hair red, as the white roots are showing a healthy two centimeters from her skull. The sister sitting in the middle, either Tamar or Yael, has thick glasses and salt-and-pepper, shoulder length, curly hair. She is overweight. The youngest one is thin and her hair is cropped short to the scalp. The three sisters are talking to their guests, who sit around on dark wooden chairs.

So many *shiva* houses. So much suffering.

I must not think that way, I remind myself, *not right now.* I am on a mission and nothing can distract me.

I spot a couple of empty chairs to the side and help myself into one. Ram joins me. I can sense his nervousness, or maybe it is something else? I didn't share with him the reason we are here, and he must be confused. Or maybe the surroundings, though unfamiliar, bring back difficult memories; the never-ending visiting men and women, the way they came in and sat quietly in front of us, exploring us with their eyes and probing with their questions.

At first, the mourning sisters do not notice us. They continue chatting with the little group of people around them. Then, "Thank you for coming," the older one says. "I'm not sure I know you. Did you know our mother? Are you from the clinic?"

I shake my head. "No, I didn't know your mother. Are you Leah?"

"Yes?" she says suspiciously.

I stand up, it is hard for me to conceal my excitement. "I'm happy to see you," I say.

Slowly, ignoring my lazy leg, I approach Leah. Her face does not show any sign of recognition. Why would she? We have never met before. She is puzzled as to who this person in front of her is. I hope she is not annoyed, but that won't matter in a second or two. I will bring her so much happiness. This must be how my stranger felt, in what seems such a long time ago.

"I'm so sorry for your loss," I say.

I put one hand on her arm, embracing her palm with my other one.

Her eyes are wide, green with streaks of hazel and one small dot of dark brown. I hold her gaze and don't let go.

All is well.

EPILOGUE

Two Years After the Shiva

RAM

For some strange coincidence, the woman suggested that they meet at Café Ness on HaYarkon Street. At first, Ram thought to reject that location, afraid to resurface the tragic memories from the night they found Nir. But then he decided it would be fine. They are meeting at a different time of the day and could sit inside. Or, he could suggest another location once they met. There were plenty of options in the area to choose from.

It was late morning when he arrived at the little coffee shop. The air smelled like rain, and the roads and sidewalks were still wet from the recent short-lived pour, probably the last one for the year, as they have already celebrated Passover. The patio looked exactly the same, with the strange collection of tables, the only seats by the picnic table. Even the lone ashtray stood there on the tabletop, ashes floated in a little puddle of rainwater. The only missing fixture was Officer Sela. Ram blinked for a second, confirming that, indeed, Sela wasn't there.

He entered the café. He had never been inside the little shop, and the first thing that struck him was how bohemian it felt. The theme of the eclectic collection of outdoor furniture continued, or to be more precise, started within. The jumble of tables, different in size and height, material and style, would drive any order-seeking person into serious anxiety. Ram ignored it and scanned the room.

"Ram?" Someone called his name from the far end of the room. "Ram, I'm so happy you came." The woman rose from her table. She zigzagged her way across the room, reaching her hand out to him. "I look different, don't I?" she said. He had seen her for a very short time while she was sitting *shiva* for her mother, but he could see now what she meant.

"Leah?"

"It's mainly my hair. I used to dye it. You probably remember me as a red-head! But I think this suits me much more." She passed a quick hand over her hair, which was now trimmed short and naturally silver.

"It's nice to see you," Ram said. He was not much for giving compliments. Leah didn't seem to mind either way.

"Come," she turned around and led the way back to her table.

When she called him on the phone the previous day, she introduced herself and reminded him of the visit he and his father gave to her *shiva* house in Herzliya. Of course he remembered, and although he asked his father more than once about it, Chaim had never explained what they were doing there. It has been almost two years since that day, and Ram was resigned to never understand.

"I'm looking for your father," she had said on the phone, and when he hesitated she added, "It's important—it *is* your father, right? The man you came with?"

"Yes, yes," he was confused. "But why are you looking for him? And why did you call me?"

"I can explain everything, but it's not for the phone."

Ram was intrigued and also happy that she contacted him first. He was still protective of his father's health, and it might be a good idea to hear first what she wanted before getting his father all excited about it. He agreed to meet as soon as she wanted, hoping she would keep up her word and not contact his father first.

"So, how did you find me?" Ram asked as they sat down by the table. "And my phone number?"

"I have my ways," she smiled. "The most important thing was when I saw your picture in the paper last week. From that point, I just needed to make a few phone calls to some good friends."

Indeed, his picture was on all the media outlets around the country. The ex-army officer now student in Tel-Aviv University who saved the life of two Palestinian toddlers who nearly drowned in the Red Sea while on his honeymoon with his new bride. He hated the media surge that came with the story, their wedding picture all over the news. He cared not for any of it.

"It's an amazing thing you did," Leah said. "And to think there are so many bad-mouthed imbeciles around this country that condemn you and wish you would have died with them… What a shame." Her face fell momentarily, and then she regained her previous merry complexion. "But I was lucky too! Finding you this way."

Her sunny personality was infectious, and Ram smiled back to her.

"I could never forget your father's face," Leah continued, "and yours too. I've been looking for you since that day. And now, I've finally found you!"

A waiter came by their table. He looked at Ram questionably, then his expression changed. "My brother!" he exclaimed, "You saved those Arabs! That's so amazing! And on your honeymoon! *Mazal tov*, brother!" He clapped Ram on the shoulder.

"Thank you," Ram smiled.

"She is beautiful, brother. You did well!" He clapped him again on the shoulder. "What's her name?"

"Tammy."

"What a lucky girl!" When Ram thought the waiter won't leave them, he finally asked, "What can I get you? It's on the house!"

Ram shuffled slightly in his chair. "No, no, I can buy my coffee. No need for—"

"Say no more, brother!" The waiter jumped on his heels and jogged to the large bar where the espresso machine stood.

Ram turned around to call after him, but Leah put her hand on his arm and said, "Let him do it. People want to reward others for their good deeds. It makes them feel good."

Ram nodded and turned back to face her.

"I want to tell you what happened that afternoon, when you and your father came to our *shiva* house."

Ram nodded again. He had a feeling that he already knew what she was about to tell him. He waited patiently for her to start.

Leah took her time. She stirred the remaining of her coffee slowly. When she finally talked, her words sounded careful, almost rehearsed. Ram couldn't blame her.

"The *shiva* for mother ended in a blur," Leah said, "and the only moment I can clearly remember was this one. It was as if the world stopped turning, the forces of life stopped ticking, and the only people left around were him and me."

Leah slowly tapped the spoon on the edge of her mug, and lay it down on its saucer. Raising her eyes, she looked directly into Ram's eyes. "If you would ask me who else came to the house, I would have to guess. My sisters would never believe me if I told them that I can't remember who visited us. It's hard for *me* to believe! You could quiz me on every student that came through my school, and I would never fail, I could name every single one, describe how they look like and what was their favorite subject. I am certain that many of my graduates have come to the *shiva*. But I can't remember a single one! Except for him. Your father."

"And me?" Ram hated to interrupt her, but he had to ask.

"And you, I guess so. But only after I saw your picture in the paper. Not before that."

Ram nodded. He let her continue telling her story.

"I only knew his first name. Chaim. But I remember everything about this particular moment. His eyes were so gentle, one smaller than the other. It blinked slower, out of tune with its partner. Even the lashes and overgrown brow on that side of his face seemed bent down and sad. A handsome nose, strong and substantial, one that says, 'I'm here and I'm not ashamed of it.'" The last bit she said in a bass tone, then chuckled. "His face was smooth-shaven, revealing the deep lines of life well lived etched there. Unlike most other men of our age, his hair was full and long, covering the top of his ears. I remember now that I thought, *How childish his hair looks!* And on top of it, a wide *kippah,* knitted and blue, decorated with a delicate design.

"I can't remember now when was the last time a religious man came to my house. Maybe a *mohel* for one of my grandchildren's circumcision ceremonies. But these were usually ultra-orthodox, dressed in black long coats and black hats. Never a man like the one in front of me.

"He asked me something, I remember that. Maybe my name. Nothing much. Then, I felt his warm palm on my arm. I don't remember seeing it rising up from his side, or reaching out to grab me, but there it was, heavy and delicate at the same time, comforting in its touch. He looked straight into my eyes, and the world ceased to exist.

"Instead of the noises and rhythm of life—the people and furniture, the walls and the street beyond them, the busy city and our sad country, torn by blood and religion—there was nothing. A blank space, a void without shapes or voices or smells. But no, it wasn't completely empty. It was blue and clear, and it was lit and warm. And he was there with me. *What happened?* I asked him without moving my lips, without uttering any sound. *Who are you?* Although at that moment everything was unknown, I felt calm as a kernel of warmth budded inside of me, spreading evenly from the depths of my stomach to each part of my body.

"*You are not alone,* I heard him say in my head. *Things are going to be all right. Don't be afraid.* Then, answering in the order I had asked, he added, *Chaim. My name is Chaim.* His hand was still holding my arm. I didn't want him to let go. *I will stay with you as long as you need.* His eyes smiled, the lazy one a bit shorter and lower than her sister. Then, without averting his gaze from me, he said, still in my head, *Look around.*

"I didn't want to take my eyes away from his. I was afraid that if I would, he would disappear, the warmth in me would die down and, even worse, would change to a freezing chill, one that will knock the life out of me. For good. When he saw how reluctant I was, he nudged me with the slightest move of the arm, pushing his chin out in the direction he wanted me to look.

"*There is nothing there,* I said, initially with full conviction, but as the words formed in my head, I knew it was not true.

"*I will not leave you,* he reassured me.

"So I turned my head, ever so slowly at first, keeping my eyes on him, making sure he would keep his promise. Then, I concentrated on the small surface of my arm where his skin touched mine. If I kept my attention on it, and my will would stay strong, he would not leave me alone there. I was sure of that. The feeling made me brave, and I finally averted my eyes away from him, looking at the direction of his protruded chin.

"Right there, behind me to my left, stood my mother."

ACKNOWLEDGMENTS

Wow —first novel published! There are so many people I would like to thank for helping me make this dream come true. It takes a village... But first, it takes a loving and supporting family.

My beloved wife, Hagit. Thank you for believing in me even when I didn't believe in myself and for always being there, suggesting ideas, feeding me when I forgot to eat and never giving up. I love you.

Daniella, Avigail, and Talia, my beautiful girls, thank you for all of your encouragements and for putting me as your role model for following your dreams. I am humbled. I can't wait see you reaching the stars.

To the team at New Degree Press who gave me the right structure to make this a reality; it's exactly what I needed. My editor, Rebecca Bruckenstein, for your amazing insights, patience, and everlasting smile and energy. The team of coaches and coauthors—you are all part of my village.

Many of the insights came from my beta readers, who helped me see where I needed to improve the story or my storytelling skills: Susan Izumi, Barry Khadalia, Sue Work, Israel Friedman, Ayala Wenner, Regan Johnson, Jaya Gupta,

Hagit, and Daniella Mikanovsky. Daniella—thank you also for introducing NaNoWriMo to me and for writing with me during November 2013, when *The Resurrector*'s journey started.

And finally, to my author community, each of you an important and unique villager! Thank you for your support, believing in me and ordering the book even before publication:

My family: Ziva and Yakov Mikanovsky, Yehudit Z"L and Moti Weinstein, Ronit and Eyal Matan, Anat and Arie Berkovits, Billy and Oren Mikanovsky, Shlomit and Yaron Flint, Merav and Moti Geva, Ami Berkovits, Bill Zahavi, Deborah Maxwell and Gerry Zahavi, Roberta Cooks, Dana and Oded Light, and Sandra and Moshe Mikanovsky.

My friends: Aakash Ahuja, Billy Anderson, Srivatsan Aravamudan, Harman Arneja, Josh Arbess, Nishit Asnani, Kathyrine Aznar, Bartosz Barcicki, Gisselle Barnhart, Rafael Bittencourt, Glenn and Hennie Black, Daniel Bloch, Andy Borchers, Mark Borndahl, Eial Boshi, Lydia Bowser, Denis Brideau, Simon Brightman, Gil Broza, Sonya Budd, Charles Bullough, Georganne Burke, Frank Caron, Peter Cebo, So Hang Chan, Billy Chen, Peter Chen, Quinnie Chen, Shaheen Chowdhury, Miriam Citron, Michael Cohen, Sorin Constantin, Cristian Contreras, Chaya Cooperberg, Martin Crawford, Nirjala Dahal, Pargles Dall'Oglio, Leticia Davolli, Tanuj Diwan, Nenita Doromal, Eric Dresdale, Elisabeth Dupree, Abe Edery, Aaron Egier, Rami El Andari, Einat Enbar, Dylan Fedy, Ashley Fico, Melissa Fleming, Israel Friedman, Sheldon Frisch, Sarah Fulton, Luis Gonzalez, Anna Geissbuhler, Atul Goyal, Matt Green, Jaya Gupta, Rick Hahn, Sammy Halabi, Thomas Hamilton, Perry Hassen, Tamara Horvath, Aaron Ingersoll, Lisa and Troy Irvine, Helen Iordanidis, Andrew Isherwood, Susan Izumi, Yasemin Kamci, Roy Karo, Eyal

Katz, Pia and Steve Katz, Emma Kaufman, Shirley Kellerstein, Wendy Kennah, Barry Khadalia, Bar Kirshon and Rony Rom, Margery and Howard Klausner, Jill and Aaron Kleid, Eric Koester, Sarah and Marty Kornblum, Jakub Kozlowski, Rashi Kuhr, Howard Kurlandski, Dena Kuzyk, May Lam, Jesse Lau, Mike Levine, Stuart Lewis, Rogerio Liparisi, Vincent Luong, Cliff Maksushimat, Thomas Maremaa, Sarah Mayberry, Kent McCrea, Jacob McMiddlebrow Mooney, Kelly Medford, Smadar Meiri, Andrew Miller, Mehrab Mirza, Sara Muir, Carrie Mumford, Mark Nagy, Ameetav Nangrani, Steven Ng, Thomas Nicholl, Phyllis Njoroge, Cliff Oliveira, Michael Oppenheimer, Priyanka Pande, Haim Peer, Ilana Pen Gudes, Jordan Pena, Timothy Peterson, Lan Phang, Deborah Potts, Mikhail Pozin, Edward Prutschi, Alexander Quirk, Debora and Ricardo Rapaport, Dave Redvers, Emily Reid, Riki Reshef-Adivi, Neil Richler, Richard Rotman, Alexander Rozov, Jennifer Rube, Claire Sacks, Lior Shalom, Shai Shandil, Joseph Sharon, Dotan Shenhav, Jenny Siede, Justin Simonelis, Gary Smith, Jake Stolee, Garland Tam, Rachel Taylor, Mark Thurgood, Jill Tomac, Graham Toppin, Dennis Turko, Howard Wasserman, Hilla Watkins, Ayala Wenner, Troy Winfrey, Priscilla Wong, Sue Work, Kevin Yanushefski, Yi Zhang, and David Zylich.

My village—thank you!